A Sweet Taste of
HISTORY

A Sweet Taste of
HISTORY

MORE THAN 100 ELEGANT
DESSERT RECIPES
FROM AMERICA'S
EARLIEST DAYS

CHEF WALTER STAIB

WITH MOLLY YUN AND DIANA WOLKOW

Photographs by Todd Trice

Foreword by David McCullough

LYONS PRESS
Guilford, Connecticut

An imprint of Globe Pequot Press

Lyons Press is an imprint of Globe Pequot Press.

Photos by Todd Trice, except for those on pages xx, 2, 5, 7, 9,
11, 13, 15, 122, 129, 133, 135, 150, and 170 by Molly Yun.

Text design and layout: Nancy Freeborn
Project editor: Ellen Urban

Library of Congress Cataloging-in-Publication Data

Staib, Walter.
A sweet taste of history : More than 100 elegant dessert recipes from America's earliest days / Chef Walter Staib with Molly Yun and Diana Wolkow ; photographs by Todd Trice.
pages cm
Summary: "From the chef and host of A Taste of History comes a beautiful cookbook that features 100 elegant dessert recipes from America's earliest days and will capture the grandeur of the sweet table—the grand finale course of an 18th century meal. At this time it was common for hostesses to arrange elaborate sweet tables that were designed as works of art. A Sweet Taste of History will blend American history with exquisite recipes and it will show the reader not only how to recreate these incredible desserts but will also discuss the importance of each one, the social story behind them, and how these dishes landed on the tables of early Americans"—
Provided by publisher.
Includes bibliographical references and index.
ISBN 978-0-7627-9143-9 (hardback)
1. Desserts. 2. Cooking, American. 3. Desserts—United States—History—18th century. 4. Cooking, American—History—18th century. I. Yun, Molly. II. Wolkow, Diana. III. Title.
TX773.S78 2013
641.86—dc23
2013027424

Printed in the United States of America
10 9 8 7 6 5 4 3 2 1

I DEDICATE THIS BOOK TO MY GRANDCHILDREN,
ISABEL, SEBASTIAN, DIEGO, AND CLOVER

Contents

Foreword

Of all those worthy patriots who gathered for the first Continental Congress in Philadelphia in late summer of 1774—and of those who later fixed their signatures to the immortal Declaration of Independence—none wrote so fully or candidly about the setting of the historic drama, or the human side of life for the protagonists, than did John Adams of Massachusetts. And quite fitting it is that Adams, describing his arrival in Philadelphia for the first time on August 29, 1774, singled out City Tavern for lavish praise. Indeed, to judge by John Adams's diary, the then-new hostelry on Second Street was the only thing about Philadelphia that made an impression that first day.

Adams and the others traveling with him had been on the road since early morning, and "dirty and dusty and fatigued" as they were, they could not resist the Tavern, where, Adams wrote, they received a "fresh welcome," "a supper . . . as elegant as ever was laid on a table." What time they sat down to eat he did not record, but it was eleven before they pushed back their chairs and called it a night, all of them, one gathers, departing amply fortified to face whatever might lay in store. For his part, Adams decided that here was the finest tavern in all America.

It was an endorsement few would have disputed, and it came from a man who dearly loved to eat, who all his life loved and appreciated good food, good drink, good talk around a convivial table.

Philadelphia in the late eighteenth century was the largest, most prosperous city in America, the busiest port, and a cornucopia without equal. Nowhere could one find such bountiful evidence of American abundance: such quantities of fresh fruit and vegetable, fresh fish, meats, sausages, wild game, and cheeses on sale; or such a variety of "elegant" cooking. Delegates from the far-flung colonies, visitors from abroad—visitors of all kinds—marveled at the produce on display at the city's enormous central market. Twice weekly, on market days, German-speaking country people rolled into the city in huge wagons laden with produce and live chickens, ducks, and pigs. One signer of the Declaration of Independence, Stephen Hopkins of Rhode Island, counted seventy farm wagons on Market Street.

In such an atmosphere, not surprisingly, minimalist cuisine was not the fashion. Dinner at City Tavern, or at any of the fine homes of Philadelphia, could include twenty or more different dishes, not counting dessert. As John Adams reported to his wife, Abigail, even "plain Quakers" served ducks, hams, chicken, and beef at a single sitting, while such desserts as served at the home of Mayor Samuel Powel on Third Street were dazzling—custards, flummery, jellies, trifles, whipped syllabubs, floating islands, fruits, nuts, everything imaginable.

But for the delegates to the Congress, City Tavern remained the great gathering place. It was there that Adams and George Washington first met. It was there that so many came and went, not yet figures in history, but flesh-and-blood human beings, let us never forget—Sam Adams, Richard Henry Lee, Patrick Henry, Thomas Jefferson, Benjamin Franklin, Dr. Benjamin Rush. And here they made history, shaped much about the world we live in, with what they said among themselves, bargaining, politicking, speaking their minds, talking small things and large over the rattle of dishes and the steady hubbub of surrounding tables. Nothing of what was said was recorded. No artist is known to have sketched such scenes.

The original City Tavern is gone. The present City Tavern, on the same site, is an exact reproduction. Still, the feeling of entering another time is strong and appealing, and it makes City Tavern a must experience for anyone with even a little interest in history—and most especially when the food comes on.

The great pull of the place is the same as long before, with the marvelous array of things to eat. Under the direction of chef/restaurateur Walter Staib, the offerings are never static, never routine, any more than in days of old, when the likes of Adams and Washington climbed the marble stairs to the front door. That this sumptuous cookbook, devoted solely to desserts and breads, contains no fewer than one hundred tantalizing receipts certainly makes the point.

The founding era of America, now more than two centuries past, was a vastly different time from our own. The people, too, were different, and more so than generally understood. Yet it is possible to make contact with them as fellow human beings. We can enter their world, we can come to know them through the letters they wrote, their diaries, the books they read, their music, their architecture, the ways they worshipped, the poetry they loved and learned by heart, and yes, God be praised, by the food they ate.

Besides, with such a guide at hand as this wonderful volume, along with its companion work, *The City Tavern Cookbook*, we are able now to enjoy such singular delights as they knew right in our own homes.

It is all well and good to read that in the eighteenth century the pleasures of the table ranked high among the pleasures of life, but quite another thing to savor the real fare itself. To dine as John Adams and his contemporaries once did at City Tavern is to be reminded of how full-flavored life at its best must have been for them, and that they themselves, at their best, were anything but dull company.

—David McCullough

Preface

I have operated the historic City Tavern for the last twenty years. It is a faithful reproduction of the original legendary Philadelphia destination established in 1773. This has given me a great understanding of the eighteenth century and what it was like to live and breathe, and to dine, in the era. My offices are located on the top floor of the building, and it's where I spend every day when I am not traveling. I walk in the steps of America's greatest founding fathers at City Tavern and in Old City, where our nation went from a colony to a country, so I feel connected to the luminaries of the era.

St. Patrick's Day 1999 was one of the most historic moments in my recent years. It was the taping of the premier of my TV show, *A Taste of History*. Looking back, we've done nearly a hundred shows, won awards, and acquired many ardent fans. Starring on the show, cooking at historic hearths around the world, and researching the recipes has given me additional insight. I've visited and cooked in some of the preeminent homes of the era—Thomas Jefferson's Monticello and George Washington's Mount Vernon, to name just two. Over the last few years, I've met with authors, scholars, historians, and interpreters. I'm amazed at their dedication and knowledge, and I've learned something new with every venture. There's always a connection between the great players of the day, the many colonies of the world, and the sweeping social and culinary movements.

I have the luxury of having many manuscripts at my fingertips because of my friend Bruce Cooper Gill, the curator and executive director of Harriton House in Bryn Mawr, Pennsylvania. I get to pore over Charles Thomson's papers and to read his own words on the developing nation. As the secretary of the Continental Congress, a close friend of Thomas Jefferson, and

a scholar and translator, he had great impact on the fledgling nation. Thomson was an abolitionist, gentleman farmer, and distiller, and he had fine taste in cuisine. His home, which was founded in 1704, also serves as the home base for filming Staib's PBS cooking show, *A Taste of History*. It was also the gorgeous and historically accurate setting for the photography in this book.

It's ironic that I also live a stone's throw away from the historic Thomson estate on property that used to be part of his dairy farm. Little did I know, when my wife, Gloria, set out to buy a new home, that she was purchasing land that was originally on this eighteenth-century estate. It was through her determination that we lived there for many years before I even came to know Bruce Cooper Gill and the treasures of Harriton House.

There was never a question in my mind that his estate would be the place for this new book to come to life. In the present day, I'm dwelling in the past and re-creating the foodways of our founding fathers, but there is no way I can know all the details. There are descriptions and paintings of sweet tables and desserts from which we learn; however, I was not actually there at some of the great feasts of the day. This is my best attempt to showcase the depth of sweets that graced the tables of the finest families in British North America as the nation was coming into its own.

There are some modern interpretations, particularly in the recipes, and because we use photographs rather than illustrations to showcase the finished products, I have tried to make the methods more approachable for today's cook with equipment that was not available to our ancestors. The photos, too, are what we imagine the sweets would have looked like and use the most authentic details possible—some are re-creations from illustrations of the era—while others are our best guesses. I wanted to bring readers many pictures so they could savor the splendor of these desserts. However, don't be intimated by the recipes or images. The embellishments are true to the eighteenth century's most elaborate parties, and I hope the reader can reflect upon and enjoy the sophistication of the taste of the latter part of the eighteenth century. But feel free to make the desserts simpler for home use, or get into the spirit and go all out with the ornamental touches shown in the book.

Many of the desserts are recognizable and still in style today and can be found at the finest resorts and restaurants. Things haven't changed so much, and we can thank the great thinkers and bakers of the 1700s for creating what we still think of as luxury. Before their era, these desserts were not popular or even possible.

The hostesses put so much thought and exacting detail into entertaining because they wanted to establish America as a nation on its own that did not pale in comparison to the older European powers. These leaders felt obliged to dispel the misconception that the new nation was a savage frontier with no refinement or taste. In their efforts to prove America's standing, the cooks and gentry established a great tradition of what would become American food that used available ingredients and Old World techniques.

Introduction

Imagine sweeping into a gilded ballroom. Feast your eyes on the dazzling display of sweets tiered in an intricate pattern on a long table against the wall. It sparkles like gems. Sugar confections tower, artfully designed cakes stand tall next to statues of sugar and ice. Long before dinner is served, the sweet table is laden and entices every sense. It is the first glimpse of decadence to come, and long after the evening is over, that unforgettable impression of indescribable sweetness and delicacy will linger.

"Hot puddings, cold puddings, steamed puddings, baked puddings, pies, tarts, creams, moulds, charlottes and bettys, trifles and fools, syllabubs and tansys, junkets and ices, milk puddings, suet puddings: 'pudding' used as a generic term covers so many dishes traditional in English cookery that the mind reels as it dwells on these almost vanished splendours of our tables," wrote Elisabeth Ayrton in her book *The Cookery of England*. We hope not to let those recipes vanish, but to bring them to life and to re-create this bygone era when elegance was at its peak and entertaining was much more than a fine art—it was a way of life for gentry.

Rather than serving something simple, hostesses arranged sweet tables that were displays of ornately cultivated beauty meant to leave guests with a lasting impression. Of course, these works of art were laden with delicious sweet edibles.

The tradition of dessert, the final course of the meal, comes from the medieval period when royalty ate sweetmeats and spiced wine to help their digestion. By the eighteenth century it had evolved into a great spectacle with grand and carefully planned arrangements of fruit, confections, cookies, cakes, and ice. This was the final and finest course of a grand meal, which would last hours, sometimes well into the night. Sweet tables were not just an afterthought but the crown jewel to the meal.

Confectioners brought a sense of humor into their arrangements by making a sweet food look like a savory dish or carving it into a spectacular beast. Ice creams were shaped to resemble fruits or vegetables—there are many illustrations of gelatins in the form of asparagus or ice creams sculpted to look like cuts of meat or animals. Leaders in the American colonies were determined to outdo the Western kingdoms they left behind, so American sweet tables became more sophisticated than some in European courts. While the founding fathers crafted democracy, they feasted on the creations of their skilled pastry chefs and the stylings of the ladies of the day. Politics were hashed over, kingdoms and counties were decided, and lives were forever changed at the table.

Americans owe much of their culinary heritage to the founding mothers. Martha Washington ran her Virginia estate, Mount Vernon, like a resort. She hosted more than five

hundred overnight guests each year and kept detailed records of what she served at parties. Her recipe for "great cake" has been modernized and is in a new cookbook. However, Martha also wrote a recipe for "an excellent cake" in her family cookbook, which she passed down to her granddaughter Nellie, who continued to cook from its pages and share it for generations.

Dolley Madison carved out a political career for her husband, James Madison, through her entertaining. Thomas Jefferson, a widower, requested that Dolley serve as his hostess at the White House. Later, when James was elected president, she threw Wednesday evening receptions where political opponents could come together to enjoy libations and camaraderie. Her lavish dinner parties were noted for the surprise delicacies served, including oyster ice cream.

There are some forgotten culinary heroines, too, such as the once-famous Elizabeth Willing Powel, the wife of the mayor of Philadelphia both before and after the Revolutionary War. Powel and his wife frequently entertained notables, including George Washington, who liked to dance and dine in their home. It was allegedly Mrs. Powel

who convinced Washington to run for a second term as president. Her sweet tables were legendary, as was her prowess at accomplishing politics over dessert.

Another impressive but overlooked woman in history was Mrs. Elizabeth Goodfellow of Philadelphia, who opened the first cooking school in America. She was a widow in a time when most single women struggled to survive. However, Mrs. Goodfellow was an excellent baker and had a good eye for business. She owned a popular bakery and sweet shop and expanded her empire into a cooking school and catering service. She catered to Philadelphia's wealthiest families, including the Powels, and taught their daughters how to cook. Mrs. Goodfellow was well known for her gingerbread and jumbles (cookies), and she is credited with the invention of the lemon meringue pie.

Hostesses of the era could either bake their own desserts or purchase them from local shops and confectioners who prided themselves on offering the best of the day. But it was not enough for desserts to be delicious; they also had to be displayed artfully. In keeping with the popular rococo style of the eighteenth century that was pervasive in architecture, art, and design, these tables were designed as total works of art. The buffets were created like tableaux with small edible sculptures, tarts, and sweetmeats. The whimsical and florid approach to fashion and art carried over to the table, and desserts lent themselves best to these scenes.

Tabletop décor was inspired by gardens in the eighteenth century, and a lady of the house would sketch out the table to create a fanciful scene. The stylish hostess would make a miniature garden tableau that would be the envy of architects and landscapers. She would accent great hedges of sweets and lanes of candies with sugar sculptures and porcelain statuettes.

The end of the eighteenth century was the beginning of America's sweet tooth. This era was significant because sugar became cheaper, more accessible, and therefore a part of daily life for common people. It was still a luxury and a means to show off status, but even servants began adding sugar to their tea and a dessert course to their meals. It was when chefs became truly creative with sugar and set the scene for centuries to come.

Beyond the famous women of the day, there were cookbook authors who remained behind in the hearth kitchen. These men and women developed "receipts," as they were named back then, and shared them with fellow cooks and hopeful hostesses. Rather than presenting the sweet table or taking credit for an elegant repast, they spent hours perfecting crusts and crumpets. Hannah Glasse, who wrote *The Art of Cookery Made Plain and Easy,* rose to great success when her book sold thousands of copies and was reprinted many times. But her work went unrecognized for decades. Because it was unseemly for a woman to publish, she was not given credit for her recipes until after her death. Her husband drove the family into debt, so she sold the rights to her book to get out of debtor's prison and didn't have a penny to show for her efforts.

Other cookbook authors began and ended their careers on higher notes, such as Mary "Molly" Randolph, a distant cousin to Thomas Jefferson, who received wealth and status for her book *The Virginia House-Wife*.

Whether the cooks and authors who remained nameless or the hostesses who were the face of sophistication, these ancestors share in the credit for establishing America's legacy of the sweet table.

CHAPTER 1

Beverages

MANY OF THE BEVERAGES POPULAR IN THE EIGHTEENTH CENTURY STILL GRACE OUR SPECIAL OCCASION MENUS. WHILE RUM PUNCH MAY BE RESERVED FOR A CARIBBEAN VACATION, BRANDY, PORT, AND CHAMPAGNE ARE ALL WELL KNOWN ON OUR DESSERT TABLES TODAY, AND EGGNOG IS A STAPLE DURING THE HOLIDAYS.

Port and, in particular, Madeira were de rigueur in America. In Britain, port was known as a cheap alternative to the Continent's wine. Britain had a trade agreement with Portugal to export its fortified wines, including Madeira, to its colonies with just a nominal duty. Ruby and tawny ports and Madeira, made especially on its namesake island in Portugal, were looked down upon in Britain, but were remarkably more tasty in the colonies. On the journey to America, Madeira swelled in its oak barrels, absorbed some of the sea air, and aged into a delicious after-dinner drink. It was by far the most popular beverage. During the French and Indian War, Benjamin Franklin wrote to propose to the committee of the assembly to give officers marching to Niagara presents of "necessaries and refreshments." These parcels included, among other consumables, "2 ounces. Old Madeira wine and 2 gallons Jamaica spirits."

Back in England, while tea became cheaper and more available to the mass population, so did gin. It was by far the most popular spirit in Britain in the mid-eighteenth century and was prevalent in the American colonies. It was mass manufactured from excess grain, doctored with juniper, and sold cheaply. Known as "British brandy," it was the poor man's drink of choice, while the upper classes preferred French brandy. Some of the names still synonymous with fine digestifs were established in the eighteenth century, including Hennessy, Gautier, and Martell.

Butlers and cooks recorded descriptions and recipes for strong dessert liqueurs that no longer exist but sound as exotic as their ingredients. There were brandies made with figs, dates, licorice, and cardamom pods. Sweet liqueurs distilled from the sundew plant, orange flowers, and citron were popular for their brilliant color and rumored aphrodisiac properties—a welcome quality for after dinner.

Rum, imported from the West Indies, was increasingly popular in American taverns and homes. Thus we settle upon one of the most fashionable beverages of the day: punch. Cocktails would not be invented until the 1920s; however, this was the grandmother of them. Fashionable punches called for brandy, rum, and fruit juices and were presented in special bowls, to be served with a ladle into "rummer" glasses.

French wines and champagnes were served with the most elegant sweet tables and accompanied

the desserts for the crème de la crème of America. Franklin later wrote in a letter in 1779, "Behold the rain which descends from heaven upon our vineyards; there it enters the roots of the vines, to be changed into wine; a constant proof that God loves us, and loves to see us happy." This was an expensive treat, so hostesses like our beloved Dolley Madison or Martha Washington would have reserved it for dinners with very important guests. Just imagine the thrill of the Marquis de Lafayette when he was served crème brûlée with a glass of bubbly from his native soil.

Ale was ubiquitous in the American colonies. Even religious groups opposed to drinking alcohol, such as the Quakers, made their own beer as a necessity. Nearly every housewife had a favorite recipe for beer that used bread yeast, a bit of sweetener, and water. Beer was boiled in the process of brewing, so it was safer to drink than water. Many new variations arose from practicality—people made beer with what they had on hand. Instead of sugar, brewers used honey or molasses. Instead of hops, clever home brewers substituted spruce sprigs or pine needles for additional flavor.

Colonists also brewed their own mead and enjoyed the sweet nectar with desserts. Mead, which is often associated with the Middle Ages, was still very popular in the eighteenth century because it was easily made on farms and estates. Beekeeping was as much a hobby back then as it was a necessary means of keeping natural sweetener on hand. Harvesting honey from beehives each year augmented the sugar supply. Sugar was an expensive ingredient that had to be imported and processed, while honey was there for the taking.

Perhaps the most common beverage in the early colonies, and later in New England and cool-weather regions, was cider. John Adams drank a tankard of hard cider every morning before starting his day. Farmers who owned small orchards made their own and kept a barrel of cider fermenting by the front door for guests to help themselves. Cookbooks of the era, even *Martha Washington's Booke of Cookery,* have recipes for women to make their own cider from peaches, persimmons, and apples at home. Large-scale orchards grafted trees for major production of apples and relied on cider sales for much of their income. James Bray III recorded sales from his Williamsburg, Virginia, plantation from 1743 to 1744—he sold 1,009 gallons of cider and 345 quarts of distilled cider in one year.

Most modern cooks won't be brewing their own ales or fermenting apple cider in casks in their root cellars. Instead, you will find recipes for beverages that hosts would have put out on special occasions, mostly simple mixtures of popular imported liquors and sweetened juices and, in the winter, warmed spirits. This cookbook does not contain anything that would require a mixologist or special methods. The phrase "cock tail" first appeared in print on May 6, 1806, in a newspaper in New York, but it was a bit of a mystery to most readers. On May 13, 1806, a letter to the editor was published with an explanation of the term, describing it as a slang term for a drink: "Cock tail, then in a stimulating liquor, composed of spirits of any kind, sugar, water and bitters it is vulgarly called a bittered sling." Cocktails remained obscure and were not popularized for decades later, growing extremely prevalent during Prohibition.

GEORGE WASHINGTON'S SMALL BEER

George Washington jotted down a recipe to brew one of his favorite types of ale. In 1757, when he put it in his personal notebook, the description was not for commercial use, but simply observations on how to make a quality porter to drink at home with friends at Mount Vernon or in an encampment with officers before battle. This dark, rich ale is delicious paired with chocolate. Could it be a coincidence that Martha's recipe for chocolate mousse is perfectly complemented by her husband's ale? Any style of porter or stout is excellent served with chocolate.

TO MAKE SMALL BEER:

> *Take a large siffer full of bran hops to your taste—Boil these 3 hours. Then strain out 30 gall n into a cooler put in 3 gall n molasses while the beer is scalding hot or rather draw the molasses into the cooler. Strain the beer on it while boiling hot, let this stand till it is little more than blood warm. Then put in a quart of ye[a]st if the weather is very cold, cover it over with a blank[et] let it work in the cask—Leave the bung open till it is almost done working—Bottle it that day week it was brewed.*

EGGNOG

Eggnog may be enjoyed exclusively during the holidays today; however, it was more akin to a protein shake to eighteenth-century travelers. It was a convenient breakfast that had nutrients to last for hours of riding and enough alcohol to keep gentlemen warm on a cold morning.

In February 1796, Isaac Weld wrote about a small entourage of travelers that stopped in Philadelphia for breakfast and enjoyed eggnog. This is the first time that the serving of eggnog was documented. The rich, filling drink of milk, eggs, rum, and sugar is as good today as it was back then. If you prefer not to serve raw eggs, use one quart of commercially prepared eggnog, which is pasteurized, as a substitute for the first three ingredients, then flavor with the remaining ingredients.

7 large egg yolks
¾ cup granulated sugar
3 cups half-and-half
1 cup bourbon
¾ cup rum
½ cup brandy
Freshly grated nutmeg, for garnish

1. In the large bowl of an electric mixer, beat together the egg yolks and sugar on high speed for about 5 minutes, until thick and pale yellow.

2. Gradually beat in the half-and-half, bourbon, rum, and brandy.

3. Cover and refrigerate until completely chilled.

4. Serve in cups or mugs. Garnish with the nutmeg.

RASPBERRY CHAMPAGNE SHRUB

MAKES 2 SERVINGS

Martha Washington and ladies of society served this beverage at their parties in the heat of the summer. This libation is perfect on a warm day because of its sweet-tart and bubbly character. Every cook had a recipe for "shrub," sweetened vinegar added to fruit. It was used to flavor and color salad dressings and beverages. Before soda existed, there was champagne shrub. For a nonalcoholic version of this drink, replace the champagne with ginger ale or club soda. It is still as refreshing as it was in the eighteenth century when served with pleasant company, even if your porch does not offer grand views of the Potomac River as the Washington's did.

¼ cup Raspberry Shrub (see page 207)

1 cup champagne or sparkling wine

1 cup ginger ale

1. Pour the shrub into a glass. Pour in the champagne and ginger ale, stirring only if the champagne fails to blend the ingredients thoroughly.

2. Serve immediately, so the champagne does not go flat.

COFFEE ROYALE

MAKES 1 SERVING

Coffee was a most controversial beverage in the eighteenth century. While commonplace on today's breakfast table, it was a thing of great expense and carried the weight of politics with it in the 1700s. Doctors of the era believed that coffee would excite nerves and incite people to extreme behavior, including overthrowing governments.

Frederick the Great, the king of Prussia, issued an edict forbidding coffee roasting, because he feared that over coffee a Prussian revolution could brew. On September 13, 1777, Frederick issued a coffee manifesto decreeing that beer was far healthier than coffee for soldiers and subjects. In place of coffeehouses, Frederick began a campaign to popularize beer halls, where he knew beer would dull the senses and calm any stirrings of insurrection among his people. In 1781, he put a royal monopoly on coffee importing and roasting. The French Revolution was largely plotted out in coffeehouses, so royal houses in other European countries grew wary. Perhaps Frederick's inclinations twelve years earlier were accurate.

1 ounce amaretto liqueur
1 ounce cognac
8 ounces hot coffee
Whipped cream, for garnish

Pour amaretto and cognac into a coffee mug and top with hot coffee. Garnish with whipped cream.

*Everybody is using coffee.
If possible, this must be prevented.
My people must drink beer.*

—FREDERICK THE GREAT

WASSAIL

MAKES 6 SERVINGS

The drink called wassail dates back to the old English custom of wassailing, or singing carols, during the Christmas and New Year's season. A big punch bowl was filled with this spiced wine, and everyone gathered around the wassail bowl to toast the season. Traditionally, groups of people would walk from house to house singing carols and reveling in the holiday season. At each house where they stopped to sing, the host would give them cups of wassail and often join the group to progress to the next house. You can imagine how warm and happy they were at the end of the night after many cups of this hot wine!

1 tablespoon grated orange rind
   (about 1 medium orange)

1 teaspoon grated lemon rind
   (about 1 medium lemon)

3 pods star anise

3 pods cardamom

10 cloves

3 sticks cinnamon

1 bottle (750 ml) red burgundy wine

¼ cup dark brown sugar

2 pinches freshly grated nutmeg

1. Place the grated orange and lemon rinds, star anise, cardamom, cloves, and cinnamon sticks into a piece of cotton cheesecloth, and tie up with kitchen twine to make a sachet.

2. Pour the wine into a large saucepan and set over low heat.

3. Place the sugar and the sachet in the wine. Add the nutmeg.

4. Heat until the wine is very warm. Do not let it boil, as boiling will burn off the alcohol content.

5. Remove from the heat and discard the sachet.

6. Serve warm.

West Indies Rum Punch

MAKES 1 SERVING

Before it was distilled in America, rum was imported through the triangular trade between West Africa, the Caribbean, and the American colonies. Merchants brought slaves from their homes in Africa to the islands, bartered for sugarcane and rum, and shipped up to New England. Rum was such an important staple in the eighteenth century that officers in the Royal Navy were paid a pint a day, and it was frequently used as currency in exotic ports of call where money could not be exchanged. This recipe combines several of the era's most popular drinks and gives a taste of warming spice.

1 cup fresh apple cider
1 ounce peach brandy
½ ounce Jamaican rum
½ ounce whiskey
1 cinnamon stick, for garnish
1 orange slice, for garnish

1. Heat the apple cider in a small saucepan over low heat until it reaches the desired temperature (this varies from person to person).

2. Pour the cider into a tall glass and add the brandy, rum, and whiskey.

3. Garnish with the cinnamon stick and orange slice and serve immediately.

Drinking Chocolate

MAKES 6 SERVINGS

Chocolate was extremely popular in the colonies, but less as a confection than as a beverage. Some recipe books include home remedies, among them drinking chocolate to cure headaches and fatigue and, for women, cramps.

John and Abigail Adams were very fond of chocolate. In 1779, John Adams, while in Spain, wrote, "Ladies drink chocolate in the Spanish fashion. Each lady took a cup of hot chocolate and drank it, and then cakes and bread and butter were served; then each lady took another cup of cold water, and here ended the repast." Abigail Adams, writing to John Quincy Adams in 1785, described drinking chocolate for breakfast while in London.

8 ounces dark chocolate, chopped

3 cups milk

¼ cup sugar

2 tablespoons cocoa powder

Cinnamon, to taste

2½ cups cream

1 teaspoon vanilla

Whipped cream, for serving, optional

1. Place the chocolate pieces in a large heatproof bowl.

2. Heat the milk over low heat in a medium saucepan. Do not bring to a boil. When heated, pour the milk over the chopped chocolate and whisk to melt the chocolate pieces.

3. In a separate saucepan, combine the sugar, cocoa, and cinnamon. Slowly whisk in the cream a little at a time, creating a thick paste and thinning the mixture as you whisk. Heat the mixture over low heat, still whisking.

4. Add the milk and chocolate mixture and the vanilla. Whisking constantly, heat the drinking chocolate until warmed through but not boiling.

5. Serve hot with whipped cream, if desired.

CHAPTER 2

Cakes

"LET THEM EAT CAKE!" IS A PHRASE THAT CALLS TO MIND BLISSFUL DECADENCE. MARIE ANTOINETTE PROBABLY NEVER UTTERED THAT PHRASE. THE FRENCH PHILOSOPHER JEAN-JACQUES ROUSSEAU REPORTED THAT A "GREAT PRINCESS" SAID IT IN 1766, WHEN MARIE ANTOINETTE WAS JUST A CHILD.

Perhaps it was her predecessor Marie-Thérèse. Although it was a commonly used phrase, it's anyone's guess who actually said it. Yet its potency remains. Cake represented all the delicacies out of reach to the commoner during the French Revolution, yet cakes were among the most popular of eighteenth-century confections in America. The grandeur of the eighteenth-century confection is within the grasp of a modern baker.

Today's cook can lay upon the table the simplest of sponge and pound cakes, as well as more elaborate and costly spice cakes, fruit-and-cream-filled trifles, and rich cheesecakes, just as colonists did.

Cakes became status symbols because of the expense of ingredients and the care taken with preparation. While many desserts were prepared by indentured servants, slaves, or hired kitchen help, cakes were often reserved for the mistress of the house. Our nation's premier hostesses, such as Lady Martha Washington and Mrs. Elizabeth Powel, had proper schooling on how to manage a household, including how to bake elegant cakes. The mistress might allow her cooks to make puddings or candies, and certainly they did the heavy lifting of the day's work, but cakes held a special place in the hearth and on the table. A gentlewoman would have closely supervised the making of cakes and attended to the icing and decorating herself.

No mishaps would have been acceptable, because the ingredients for these cakes were expensive and hard to come by, and many of the original recipes called for large quantities to feed a crowd. Martha Washington ordered up dozens of eggs and an entire peck of flour for her cake, while Hannah Glasse often called for pounds of butter!

Like today's finest baking instructors, those of the eighteenth century emphasized that understanding basic techniques was essential to preparing successful cakes. Some, like Elizabeth Raffald, author of *The Experienced English Housekeeper*, wrote clear instructions in her chapter on cakes that applied to the recipes that followed. Today's bakers would benefit as much from these suggestions that are more than two hundred years old as they would from any other:

OBſERVATIONS UPON CAKES

When you make any Kind of Cakes, be ſure that you get your Things ready before you begin, then beat your Eggs well, and don't leave them 'till you have finiſhed the Cakes, or elſe they will go back again, and your Cakes will not be light; if your Cakes are to have Butter in, take Care you beat it to a fine Cream before you put in your Sugar, for if you beat it twice the Time, it will not anſwer ſo well. . . . bake all Kinds of Cake in a good Oven, according to the Size of your Cake, and follow the Directions of your Receipt, for though Care hath been taken to Weigh and Meaſure every Article belonging to every Kind of Cake, yet the Management and the Oven muſt be left to the Maker's Care.

Benjamin Franklin's Parmesan Cheesecake

MAKES 1 (8-INCH) CAKE

One of the best-known inventors and statesmen, Benjamin Franklin created many of his innovations in his home in Philadelphia. He established the post office, where he served as postmaster general, developed hospitals, founded fire companies, and printed *Poor Richard's Almanac*. But it was while traveling abroad that Franklin made many of his culinary discoveries.

Franklin often wrote to his friend John Bartram, a well-respected horticulturist who established America's first botanical garden on the outskirts of Philadelphia. Franklin sent seeds to Bartram with descriptions of the plants and what to do with the vegetables. In 1770 when he was in London, he wrote to Bartram about soybeans, which he called Chinese caravances, and how to make "Tau-fu" with them.

Beyond being the father of tofu in America, Franklin reported to his friend about a vastly popular cheese that caught on quickly: Parmesan. In 1769 Franklin was traveling in Italy and wrote, "And for one I confess that if I could find in any Italian Travels a Receipt for making Parmesan Cheese, it would give me more Satisfaction than a Transcript of any Inscription from any Stone whatever."

It took four years, but in 1773 Franklin received a letter explaining the process of making his favorite aged cheese. This recipe plays ode to Franklin's love of cheese and his fondness for eating desserts. This cheesecake would be lovely served with an aged sherry, just as the great man himself may have enjoyed it.

CRUST

1½ cups graham cracker crumbs

½ cup finely chopped walnuts

½ cup grated Parmesan cheese

2 tablespoons granulated sugar

4 ounces (1 stick) unsalted butter, melted

CAKE

1¼ cups grated Parmesan cheese

6 ounces cream cheese, at room temperature

2 ounces sour cream

2 eggs, separated

½ cup granulated sugar

1 teaspoon lemon juice

½ teaspoon lemon zest

1. Preheat the oven to 350°F. Grease an 8-inch springform pan.

2. Prepare the crust: In a medium-sized mixing bowl, mix the dry ingredients. Toss together with the melted butter and press into the bottom and 1½ inches up the sides of the greased pan.

3. Bake for 8 to 10 minutes or until the top edge of the crust begins to brown. Let it cool on a wire rack while you prepare the filling. Keep the oven on.

4. Prepare the cake: With a wooden spoon or spatula in a medium-sized bowl, mix the Parmesan, cream cheese, sour cream, egg yolks, sugar, lemon juice, and lemon zest until incorporated and smooth.

5. In the clean and dry bowl of an electric mixer with the whip attachment, beat the egg whites to stiff peaks.

6. Gently fold the whites into the cheese mixture, pour into the crust, and bake for 25 to 30 minutes until the edges are slightly puffed and the center is mostly set. (A little wobble in the center when you bump the pan is okay.)

7. Remove and cool completely on a wire rack. Refrigerate for at least 4 hours before serving.

BENJAMIN FRANKLIN'S PARMESAN CHEESECAKE

BLACKBERRY ALMOND CHEESECAKE
MAKES 1 (10-INCH) CAKE

Eighteenth- and nineteenth-century cookbooks commonly included cheesecake recipes that date to the fifteenth century. Today we are most familiar with cheesecakes made from either cream cheese or ricotta. During the eighteenth century, however, all of these cakes called for a cheese the consistency of ricotta or cottage cheese, which was beaten smooth and often pushed through a fine sieve to create an even silkier texture.

Although cheese was available for purchase, period recipes detail the cheese-making process, suggesting that many home cooks did, in fact, prepare their own. It goes without saying that any household with dairy cows and an abundance of milk could have made soft, creamy cheese at home and saved their money for items they could not readily make, such as refined sugar or spices.

Unlike cheesecakes today, eighteenth-century varieties nearly always called for the additional textures and flavors of crushed macaroons, almonds, Naples biscuits (similar to ladyfingers), and nutmeg. In keeping with those popular additions, this cheesecake has toasted almonds for additional texture. It becomes a showstopping dessert, however, with the addition of the blackberry mixture swirled in at the last moment just before baking. Serve this whole on a pretty cake stand to impress even the most discriminating guest. The purple-hued swirls contrast with the creamy white cheesecake filling to make a gorgeous cake that will stand out on any sweet table.

CRUST

1 cup graham cracker crumbs
½ cup almonds, toasted and chopped
¾ cup granulated sugar
1 teaspoon cinnamon
Pinch of salt
4 ounces (1 stick) butter, melted and
   cooled slightly

1. Preheat the oven to 325°F. Spray a 10-inch springform pan with nonstick spray.

2. Stir together the dry ingredients.

3. Stir in the butter and mix until all crumbs are moistened.

4. Press the mixture into the bottom of the prepared pan, and flatten with a flat-bottomed glass.

5. Bake the crust for 5 to 10 minutes, or until it just starts to brown around the edges. Cool to room temperature.

CUSTARD

3 pounds cream cheese, at room temperature

2 cups granulated sugar

¼ cup sour cream

2 tablespoons almond extract

6 extra-large eggs

¾ cup blackberry puree

1. Preheat the oven to 275°F.

2. Bring a large pot of water to boil.

3. With the paddle attachment, mix the cream cheese and sugar together in the bowl of an electric mixer on speed 1 until completely smooth. Scrape down the sides of the bowl and the paddle often to ensure that there will be no lumps; after this first step, there is no way to remove lumps.

4. Add the sour cream and almond extract; mix again on speed 1 to combine, and scrape down the sides of the bowl.

5. Add the eggs, one at a time, scraping down the sides of the bowl after each addition.

6. Pour two-thirds of the custard over the crust and set aside.

7. Mix the remaining one-third of the custard with the blackberry puree, then pour it over the custard in the pan and swirl with a toothpick.

8. Place the cheesecake pan in a large roasting pan. Fill the roasting pan with the boiling water so that the water comes halfway up the sides of the cheesecake pan. This creates a water bath for the cheesecake to bake evenly. Carefully transfer to the oven and bake for 45 minutes.

9. Check the cheesecake, rotate the pan if you notice uneven browning, and return it to the oven in its water bath to bake for another 30 minutes. You'll know the cheesecake is done when the top is evenly matte and the custard does not wobble.

10. Remove the cheesecake from the water bath and place on a rack to cool completely at room temperature.

11. Refrigerate the cheesecake for at least 1 hour before unmolding.

GINGERBREAD

MAKES 1 (9 X 13-INCH) CAKE OR BUNDT CAKE

Gingerbread's history in the West dates back to when European traders first plied the Silk Road and brought back exotic spices. Chinese recipes for this spicy sweet emerged in the tenth century, and by the Middle Ages Europeans had developed versions of their own.

Ever popular in England, gingerbread naturally remained in fashion in colonial America. Recipes commonly appear in eighteenth- and early-nineteenth-century American "receipt" or recipe books. Some recipes contained orange zest and juice, while others called for lemon.

Quite a few books, like M. E. Rundell's *A New System of Domestic Cookery*, provide more than one variety; among the four this author included in her book were "A good plain sort" and "A good sort without butter."

Gingerbread was an elegant dessert to serve in the eighteenth century. In fact, Mary Ball Washington, George Washington's mother, served her version of gingerbread to the Marquis de Lafayette when he visited her home in Fredericksburg, Virginia. That recipe was passed down through generations of the Washingtons and became lovingly known as Lafayette Gingerbread.

6 ounces (1½ sticks) unsalted butter

1 cup light brown sugar

¼ teaspoon salt

⅔ cup molasses

½ teaspoon grated orange zest

1 egg

2⅔ cups all-purpose flour

1½ teaspoons baking powder

½ teaspoon baking soda

2½ teaspoons ground ginger

1¼ teaspoons ground cinnamon

¾ teaspoon ground allspice

½ teaspoon ground cloves

⅔ cup buttermilk

1. Preheat the oven to 350°F and fit a piece of parchment into the bottom of a cake pan, or grease the sides and bottom of a Bundt pan.

2. In the bowl of an electric mixer with the paddle attachment, beat the butter, sugar, and salt until light and fluffy, scraping down often. Add the molasses and orange zest and beat until incorporated.

3. With the mixer running, add the egg, then scrape down the bowl.

4. Sift the dry ingredients together. With the mixer on a slow speed, add the dry ingredients alternately with the buttermilk to the butter mixture, scraping down often.

5. Spread the batter in pan and bake 20–25 minutes for a 9 × 13 cake pan, 30–40 minutes for a Bundt pan, or until the cake is golden and puffed and a toothpick inserted comes out clean.

POUND CAKE

MAKES 1 (9 X 5-INCH) LOAF

Nearly every recipe book in colonial America included a recipe for this cake. Because they were ever interested in incorporating exotic spices into baked goods, it is hardly surprising that most eighteenth-century recipe writers suggested adding caraway seeds as well. Other variations use this same recipe and ratio of ingredients as a base to build upon, adding candied fruits or diverse spices to make a dense yet flavorful cake. Feel free to add your own touch to this recipe, as any eighteenth-century cook would do. Toss in a teaspoon of almond or anise flavoring, or add a bit of lemon juice, to your taste.

Pound cake gets its name from the quantities of ingredients—a pound each of butter, sugar, eggs, and flour. This recipe, like most contemporary interpretations of the traditional favorite, alters the original ratio of ingredients to achieve a somewhat lighter, easier-to-prepare cake. It is a "good keeper" and will last for several days because it is dense and rich and remains moist. Some recipes claim it is better if it rests for a day or two after being baked. Pound cake is not so en vogue as it was in the eighteenth century, or even in the late nineteenth and early twentieth century, when every homemaker kept a loaf or two in the pantry to serve to unexpected callers. Pound cake complemented the coffee, tea, or spiritous beverages that often accompanied it on the eighteenth-century sweet table or tea table, and it still does today.

1 pound (4 sticks) unsalted butter, softened

2 cups granulated sugar

$\frac{2}{3}$ teaspoon salt

5 eggs

1 egg yolk

2¼ cups cake flour

1⅓ teaspoons baking powder

1 teaspoon vanilla extract

1. Preheat oven to 375°F. Grease a 9 × 5-inch loaf pan and line it with parchment.

2. In the bowl of an electric mixer with the paddle attachment, beat together the butter, sugar, and salt until light and fluffy, scraping down the sides of the bowl often.

3. With the mixer running on medium speed, incorporate the eggs and yolk, one at a time, scraping down between each addition.

4. Sift together the flour and baking powder, add to the mixer bowl, and mix on low speed until 90 percent incorporated.

5. With the mixer running on low speed, pour in the vanilla extract and mix until just combined.

6. Pour into the prepared loaf pan and bake 45 minutes to 1 hour, or until the cake is golden brown and a toothpick inserted comes out clean.

Ricotta Cheesecake

MAKES 1 (10-INCH) CAKE; SERVES 10–12

Ricotta cheese has been a popular ingredient in both savory and sweet dishes for hundreds of years. Italian dessert course menus dating back to the 1660s include creamy ricotta served alongside Muscat grapes, "pears of every sort," prunes, and honeyed cream in wafers.

This recipe is inspired by the many cheesecakes that appeared in period cookbooks. More than merely creamy confections, these cakes were often elaborately flavored compositions that took advantage of many imported ingredients, such as the spices, fruits, and wine included in this version.

This is not the standard New York cheesecake now found in delis and on menus across America, but a much more interesting version. It is the grandmother to the rather bland generation of cheesecakes we know today, when cooks have omitted all but cheese, sugar, and crumbs.

ALMOND SHORT CRUST

9 ounces (2 sticks plus 2 tablespoons) unsalted butter, softened

¾ cup confectioners' sugar

2½ cups all-purpose flour, sifted

½ teaspoon salt

¾ teaspoon vanilla extract

⅙ teaspoon orange flower water

¼ cup sliced almonds

RICOTTA FILLING

¾ cup granulated sugar

½ cup honey

4½ cups (40 ounces) ricotta cheese

½ cup cake flour

4 large egg yolks

3 large whole eggs

½ cup whole milk

1 tablespoon vanilla extract

1 teaspoon almond extract

1 lemon, zest grated

1 orange, zest grated

1 teaspoon ground nutmeg

1 teaspoon ground cinnamon

½ teaspoon ground cardamom

¼ cup finely chopped apricot, soaked overnight in ¼ cup Madeira wine

¼ cup golden raisins, soaked overnight in ¼ cup Madeira wine

1. Preheat oven to 375°F.

2. Prepare the crust: In the bowl of an electric mixer fitted with the paddle attachment, cream the butter and sugar until light and fluffy.

3. Scrape down the sides of the bowl, add in the flour and salt, and carefully mix until moistened.

4. Drizzle in vanilla and orange flower water and mix a few turns

5. Add in almonds and mix until combined.

6. Transfer dough into greased and parchment-lined springform (or cheesecake) pan and press into the bottom and 1 inch up the sides as evenly as possible. Freeze for 5 to 10 minutes.

7. Line dough with parchment or foil, fill with pie weights, and bake 10 minutes until crust begins to brown.

8. Remove weights and liner and bake an additional 10 to 15 minutes, or until the entire crust is golden and firm to the touch. Cool completely on a wire rack.

9. Prepare the ricotta filling: Whisk the sugar and honey into the ricotta cheese. Sift the cake flour over cheese mixture and whisk it in.

10. Add the egg yolks and whole eggs in three additions, whisking thoroughly after each. Whisk in the milk, vanilla and almond extracts, then the lemon and orange zests, nutmeg, cinnamon, and cardamom.

11. Stir in the soaked apricots and soaked raisins, then pour the filling into the cooled crust.

12. Reduce the oven temperature to 300°F and bake until the cake is golden and a toothpick inserted in the center comes out clean.

13. Cool the cake completely on a wire rack, then unmold. Serve at room temperature or chilled.

ORANGE GLAZED ALMOND CAKE

MAKES 1 (9-INCH-SQUARE) CAKE

Recipe books of the eighteenth and nineteenth centuries commonly referred to frangipane as almond cake or French almond cake. America, like England, imported almonds from Spain, and Spanish almonds were often referred to as Jordan almonds in that era. Bitter almonds, considered poisonous and now illegal in the United States, were also frequently used in almond cake, although peach kernels were considered an acceptable substitute.

Almond cakes were served either plain or, like Eliza Leslie's version in her popular cookbook, *Receipts for Pastry, Cakes, and Sweetmeats,* with iced lemon-flavored meringue. However, this recipe relies on another popular yet exotic fruit—oranges.

Almond cake was one of the simplest of confections, consisting of four or five ingredients: almonds, flour, eggs, sugar, and lemon essence. We are reminded once again, however, that eighteenth-century baking was a time-consuming and labor-intensive task. Almond paste was available but very expensive, so cooks often chose to process almonds themselves.

Martha Washington explained this procedure clearly: one almond cake called for "a quarter of a pound of almonds, blanched in well water, & beaten in rose water." The other ingredients required refining as well. Sugar was mostly available in hard lumps or cones, so these recipes often called for "loaf-sugar, powdered and sifted" and "fine flower, well dryed against ye fire." In addition, it would have taken quite a few hours to heat an oven and usually another hour or so to bake the cake.

George Washington loved oranges from his first mention of them in his diary when he went to Barbados with his brother as a teenager. As an adult, he ordered them by the dozens from the West Indies, often as a gift for Martha. The gentleman farmer developed methods to grow his own with the help of his greenhouse, where the trees survived the Virginia winters.

CAKE

14 ounces almond paste

9 large eggs, divided

12 ounces (3 sticks) unsalted butter, room temperature

¾ cup granulated sugar

¾ teaspoon vanilla extract

1 cup cake flour, sifted

¾ teaspoon salt

⅔ cup sliced almonds, toasted, for decoration

GLAZE

1½ cups confectioners' sugar, sifted

¼ cup fresh-squeezed orange juice

Zest of ½ orange, or to taste

1. Preheat oven to 350°F. Grease a 9 × 9-inch pan and line it with parchment paper.

2. In the bowl of an electric mixer with the paddle attachment, beat the almond paste and 2 eggs until smooth, scraping down the sides of the bowl often.

3. Add the butter and sugar, and cream them until light and fluffy, scraping down the sides of the bowl often.

4. Add the vanilla and remaining eggs one at a time, scraping down the sides of the bowl between each addition.

5. Add the flour and salt and mix until just combined.

6. Pour into the prepared pan. Bake 15 to 20 minutes until the top is lightly browned and a toothpick inserted comes out clean.

7. Cool in the pan on a wire rack for 10 minutes before inverting onto a plate and cooling completely.

8. For the glaze, whisk all ingredients together in a small bowl.

9. Pour over the cooled cake and top with toasted almond slices.

Mary Randolph's Shrewsbury Cakes

MAKES APPROXIMATELY 1 DOZEN

Mary Randolph, familiarly known as Molly to her family and close friends, was a distant cousin to Thomas Jefferson. Although Molly's husband and Thomas Jefferson deeply disputed politics, she was often a guest at Monticello. The Randolph women had a large legacy of housekeeping, maintaining a well-stocked pantry, preparing menus, and reading extravagant recipes to the slaves in the kitchen. Cousin Mary wrote down many of these trade secrets in *The Virginia House-Wife* for other women to more easily manage a household expected to accommodate and entertain large families and visiting dignitaries who might dine for several days with the family. Her book went on to become one of the most influential cookbooks of the era.

Her Shrewsbury cakes are not the soft, fluffy creations we call cakes today but more closely resemble a sweet biscuit or scone. She recommends making individual cakes in "pretty shape," and cutting them out using cookie cutters, a round biscuit cutter, or freehand with a knife. These sweet but spicy little cakes would be ideal served with afternoon tea. Even better, do Mrs. Randolph and her family of Virginia gentry proud: Use them as a crowning finish to a southern-style brunch.

Molly Randolph certainly didn't invent Shrewsbury cakes, although her addition of coriander is wonderful. Coriander is the seed for the leafy green cilantro. It is most commonly used today for spicing curries, brines, and other savory and exotic dishes. It adds a pleasant flavor that will keep guests guessing.

Another recipe for Shrewsbury cakes comes from a delightful "booke of cookerie" printed in 1621, *A Daily Exercise for Ladies and Gentlewomen.* The author, "John Murrell, professor thereof," instructs the cook that she can bake them well in advance: "you may keep them halfe a yeare but new baked are best." Although his suggestion may have been timely in the seventeenth century, we recommend baking them no more than one day before serving. They are divine served with tea in the British style with clotted cream and jam.

1 egg

1 egg yolk

3 tablespoons melted butter

1 ounce brandy

½ cup granulated sugar

1¾ cups all-purpose flour

1½ teaspoons ground coriander

1. Preheat oven to 300°F.

2. In the bowl of an electric mixer with the paddle attachment, beat the egg, yolk, and melted butter until creamy.

3. With the mixer on low speed, stream in the brandy.

4. Whisk together the remaining ingredients in a small bowl and slowly add them to the butter mixture, mixing at a low speed until a dough ball forms.

5. Turn the dough out onto a lightly floured surface and roll slightly thicker than ¼ inch.

6. Cut into decorative shapes using cookie cutters or a knife, place on a parchment-lined baking sheet, and bake for 10 to 12 minutes or until firm to the touch. There should be no more than a hint of browning around the edge of the cakes.

7. Cool to room temperature and serve with preserves, tea, and/or clotted cream.

HANNAH GLASSE'S SAFFRON CAKE

MAKES 1 (10-INCH) CAKE

In her book *The Art of Cookery Made Plain and Easy*, Hannah Glasse instructs:

> You muſt take a quarter of a peck of fine flour, a pound and a half of butter, three ounces of caraway-ſeeds, six eggs beat well, a quarter of an ounce of cloves and mace beat together, a pennyworth of cinnamon beat, a pound of ſugar, a pennyworth of roſe-water, a pennyworth of ſaffron, a pint and a half of yeaſt, and a quart of milk ; mix it all together lightly with your hands thus : firſt boil your milk and butter, then ſkim off the butter, and mix with your flour, and a little of the milk ; ſtir the yeaſt into the reſt and ſtrain it, mix it with the flour, put in your ſeed and ſpice, roſe-water, tincture of ſaffron, ſugar, and eggs ; beat it all up well with your hands lightly, and bake it in a hoop or pan, but be ſure to butter the pan well : it will take an hour and a half in a quick oven. You may leave out the ſeed if you choose, and I think it rather better without it; but that you may do as you like.

Saffron was as impressive in the eighteenth century as it is today. It was and continues to be one of the most expensive culinary spices because harvesting it is so labor intensive. It is derived from the crocus flower, and it takes 75,000 flowers to make one pound of saffron. Each purple crocus provides only three stigmas (threads), which must be hand-picked immediately after opening the flower.

Saffron's flavor is released by heat, so it's no wonder that Hannah suggests heating the milk with the saffron before adding it to the batter. Modern-day cooks combine saffron with a dash or two of very hot water and let stand for 10 minutes before using. Today this fragrant spice is integral to dishes like bouillabaisse and paella, but it is seldom used in desserts. This recipe is as pretty as it is delicious, thanks to the interesting addition of saffron. This cake uses yeast as its leavening agent and is not intended to be very sweet. It is perfect for use in a trifle, or on its own served with a sugar glaze or dusted with confectioners' sugar.

2 cups whole milk

1½ teaspoons saffron threads

4 cups all-purpose flour

1 cup granulated sugar

1 teaspoon ground cloves

½ teaspoon ground mace

9 ounces (2 sticks plus 2 tablespoons) cold unsalted butter, cubed

1 tablespoon instant active dry yeast

3 eggs

½ teaspoon rose water

1. In a small saucepan over medium heat, bring the milk to a simmer. Add the saffron and remove from the stove. Stir occasionally.

2. In the bowl of an electric mixer with the paddle attachment, mix the flour, sugar, spices, and butter on medium-low speed until the butter is broken into pea-sized bits and the mixture resembles wet sand.

3. Dissolve the yeast in the warm saffron milk. The milk should be warm to the touch at this point (you should be able to have your hands in it without burning them); if the milk is too hot it will kill the yeast.

4. With the mixer running on medium speed, add the eggs and rose water. Scrape down the sides of the bowl and the paddle.

Then slowly stream in the milk mixture, scrape again, and mix until just combined.

5. Grease a 10-inch cake pan and line it with parchment. Pour the dough into the pan, cover with plastic wrap, and set in a warm place to rise for 30 minutes, or until the pan is three-quarters full.

6. Preheat the oven to 350°F, gently remove the plastic wrap, and place the pan in the middle of the oven. Bake for approximately 1 hour or until the cake is golden brown on top and a toothpick inserted comes out clean.

7. Cool in the pan on a wire rack for 10 minutes before turning out onto a plate to cool completely.

Martha Custis Washington's Excellent Cake

MAKES 1 (10-INCH 4-LAYER) CAKE

From Martha Washington's *Booke of Cookery:*

To Make an Excellent Cake

Take a peck of flowre, 10 eggs beaten, 2 nutmegg, A quartern of cloves & mace, 2 pound & halfe of fresh butter, one pound of sugar, 6 pound of currans. wash, dry, & pick them very well. then take halfe a pownd of candyed orring, leamon, & citron pill, & mince it small. & make a possit with good cream, halfe A pinte of sack, & as much Ale. & put halfe of yr butter into ye posset & ye other halfe with some good ale barme. put in to ye flowre & break it in, into small bits, & strow in some rose w[ater, juice of lea] mond, & sack as you mingle & knead up. A little ambergreece in ye Jack.

This cake is a longtime pursuit of Chef Staib's, and it all happened as if it were meant to be. Many people are familiar with some of Martha's other cake recipes, including her famous "great cake." However, Chef Staib was in search of a more unique eighteenth-century dessert for years. When filming his TV show, *A Taste of History*, he had the rare opportunity to shoot a scene while holding Martha's original book of cookery that is housed in the Pennsylvania Historical Society located just blocks from City Tavern restaurant.

Chef Staib held the book in his hands, opened it carefully, and it fell upon a page in her section on desserts. It opened to this very recipe, To Make an Excellent Cake. Caught on camera by the film crew, it was as if Martha herself were in the room guiding the book in his hands.

Her recipe, unlike many modern cakes, calls for yeast and ale. More similar to bread, it must rise before baking. Served on its own, the excellent cake is more like a scone and is delicious served with tea. However, Staib took it one step further with a rum simple syrup to moisten it and an orange buttercream icing, which is not in Martha's original book. She perhaps would have glazed her cake or served it with a meringue icing. However, to make a true centerpiece, a cake worthy of cover art, Chef Staib highly recommends the decadent buttercream icing and dried orange sections for garnish.

It is documented that George Washington gave Martha the gift of oranges at least twice in their marriage, and we believe this treatment of her cake recipe will be a gift to your guests.

1 cup ale, divided

1 ounce active yeast

1 cup heavy cream

¼ cup sherry

8 cups all-purpose flour

1 teaspoon ground nutmeg

½ teaspoon ground cloves

½ teaspoon ground mace

1 cup granulated sugar

12 ounces (3 sticks) unsalted butter, cold

2 eggs

1 egg yolk

1 tablespoon rose water

1 tablespoon lemon juice

1½ pounds currants

2 ounces candied orange peel, chopped

1. Preheat the oven to 340°F.

2. Spray two 10-inch cake pans with nonstick spray and line with parchment paper.

3. Make a barm: Warm ½ cup ale and dissolve the yeast in it. Let sit about 5 minutes or until the yeast begins to froth in the ale.

4. Mix the heavy cream, sherry, and remaining ½ cup ale in a large bowl.

5. In the bowl of an electric mixer fitted with the paddle attachment, mix the flour, spices, and sugar at a low speed. Then cut in the butter until pea-sized bits remain and the mixture resembles wet sand.

6. Slowly add the barm, the cream-sherry-ale mixture, eggs, egg yolk, rose water, and lemon juice while the mixer is running. Beat until combined on low speed.

7. Using a wooden spoon, stir in the currants and orange peel by hand.

8. Cover the bowl with plastic wrap and allow the dough to rise for 1 hour, or until doubled in volume, in a warm place.

9. Divide the dough in half and press each half into the prepared 10-inch round cake pans. Cover with plastic wrap and allow the dough to rise in a warm place until the pans are three-quarters full, about 1 hour.

10. Gently remove the plastic wrap and bake the cakes for about 45 to 60 minutes, or until a toothpick comes out clean.

BUTTERCREAM ICING

2½ pounds confectioners' sugar

2 cups egg whites

2 pounds (8 sticks) unsalted butter

Zest of 2 oranges

Candied orange peel for garnish, optional

1. Place the sugar and egg whites in the heatproof bowl of an electric mixer. Set the bowl over a pan of gently simmering water, and whisk until the sugar has dissolved and the egg whites are hot to the touch, about 3 minutes. The mixture should be completely smooth.

2. Transfer the bowl to the mixer stand. Using the whisk attachment, beat on high speed until the mixture has cooled completely and formed stiff and glossy peaks, about 10 minutes.

3. Cut the butter into ½-inch pieces and add it, one piece at a time, beating until incorporated after each addition. Add the zest, and slowly whisk to combine.

TEA SIMPLE SYRUP

¾ cup granulated sugar
1 cup water
1 black tea bag
1 ounce spiced rum
1 teaspoon rose water

1. In a small saucepan, bring the sugar and water to a boil. Remove from heat.

2. Add the tea bag and let it steep for 5 minutes, or until it turns the syrup brown.

3. Remove the tea bag and stir in the rum and rose water. Let stand at room temperature until ready to use; can be made up to 3 days in advance.

ASSEMBLY

1. Using a serrated knife, slice the rounded top off each cake, making it level and flat.

2. Slice each cake in half horizontally, making two layers from each pan, being careful to keep the layers as even as possible. You will end up with four even round layers.

3. Brush each layer with the tea simple syrup, generously coating each one so that it absorbs the moisture and flavor.

4. Place one layer on a cake stand or plate. Top with orange buttercream, spreading the icing to the edge. Repeat with the other layers, building a four-layer cake.

5. Finish the cake by icing the top and sides with the orange buttercream.

6. Garnish with candied orange peel or dehydrated orange slices, if desired.

PLUM CAKE

MAKES 1 (10-INCH) CAKE

Wild plums grew plentifully in the New World, and, as was the case with many fruits, new varieties developed as settlers cultivated plum stones brought to American shores from Europe. George Washington at Mount Vernon and Thomas Jefferson at Monticello grew American and European plums and would have enjoyed them fresh in the late summer, dried in the fall, and in sweetened preserves in the winter.

There are hundreds of varieties of plums available today, each one with its own rich color, distinct flavor, and ideal cooking method. Choose the prettiest plums you can find for this recipe, and enjoy as the juicy slices bake for a stained-glass effect atop the cake.

With the exception of plum preserves, all eighteenth-century plum recipes call for raisins or currants (or both) rather than plums. Since the Middle Ages, the word "plum" was used not only for a particular sort of fresh fruit but also as a general term for small dried fruit. Cookbook writers, like their audiences, knew that raisins and currants were dried grapes, but perhaps the similarities between the dried fruits led to this general use.

Like many authors, Amelia Simmons included a recipe for "plumb cake" in her cookbook *American Cookery*, which called for currants rather than plums. Although the dried fruit was incorporated into the sweetened yeast dough instead of mixed with a topping, the ingredients in her recipe reveal a similarity to this one.

This dessert is not too sweet, so it is ideal served with coffee for a midday reprieve or late-morning picker-upper. One can just imagine fine ladies of the 1700s gathered round in a drawing room trading gossip of the day, sipping tea and the newly popular coffee drink, while tasting this type of cake.

SWEET DOUGH

2 cups all-purpose flour
4 tablespoons (½ stick) unsalted butter, at room temperature
2 tablespoons honey
¼ teaspoon salt
¼ cup whole milk, at room temperature
1 large egg
2 large egg yolks
½ tablespoon active dry yeast

TOPPING

7 large plums
1 cup (8 ounces) sour cream
3 tablespoons honey
Zest of 1 lemon
¼ cup light brown sugar
Pinch of ground cardamom
1 teaspoon ground cinnamon
1½ cups slivered almonds
2 tablespoons unsalted butter, melted
Whipped cream for serving, optional

1. Prepare the dough: In the bowl of an electric mixer fitted with the dough hook attachment, place the flour, butter, honey, and salt. Mix together on low speed until butter is in pea-sized pieces and combined with other ingredients.

2. In a small mixing bowl, whisk together the milk, egg, yolks, and yeast, and add these wet ingredients to the electric mixer bowl. Mix on low speed for 4 minutes. Increase the speed to medium and mix for another 4 minutes, or until the dough pulls away from and slaps against the sides of the bowl.

3. Cover the dough with plastic wrap and allow it to rise in a warm place until doubled in volume, about 1 hour.

4. Prepare the topping: Slice the plums in half and remove the pits. Slice each half into thirds. Set the plums aside.

5. In a medium-sized mixing bowl, whisk together the sour cream, honey, and lemon zest. Set aside.

6. In a smaller bowl, stir together the brown sugar, cardamom, and cinnamon. Set aside.

7. Grease a 10-inch round springform pan pan with butter, and coat lightly with flour. Once the dough has doubled in volume, punch it down and press it into the bottom of the prepared cake pan.

8. Spread the sour cream mixture atop the dough. Sprinkle the almonds over the sour cream, and arrange the sliced plums nicely on top. Brush the sliced plums with the melted butter, and dust the top of the cake with the sugar mixture.

9. Allow the dough to rest for 30 minutes. Preheat the oven to 375°F.

10. Bake for 40 minutes, or until the plums have caramelized and a toothpick inserted comes out clean. Let the cake cool in the pan for 20 minutes, and then transfer onto a serving plate. The cake can be served either warm or at room temperature. Serve with whipped cream, if desired.

MARTHA WASHINGTON'S CHOCOLATE MOUSSE CAKE

MAKES 1 (10-INCH) CAKE

George Washington had a fondness for chocolate. Records at Mount Vernon reveal he first ordered chocolate from England in 1757, and he received twenty pounds a year later.

Correspondence between the general and his guests reflects that he served chocolate as a special beverage to them during his presidency.

Washington famously advocated for American government to be very unlike a monarchy and for its principal players to have different titles than royalty, such as *president*. However, during the Revolutionary War, Washington's soldiers referred to Martha as the General's Lady. The title "Lady Washington" stuck. Of course, she went on to become the first First Lady. In her *Booke of Cookery*, Martha details the technique to make a fluffy chocolate mousse. This would have been reserved for dinners in the winter, because it surely would have slumped and melted in the Virginia summer, even with the help of spring houses to keep it cool. Her mousse is sandwiched between two layers of chocolate sponge cake, a very popular serving method of the day.

CHOCOLATE SPONGE CAKE

2½ cups cake flour

1½ cups cocoa powder

8 egg yolks

1½ cups plus 2 tablespoons granulated sugar, divided

⅔ cup vegetable oil

8 ounces cold water

1 tablespoon vanilla extract

4 teaspoons baking powder

1 teaspoon salt

8 egg whites

1. Preheat the oven to 325°F. Grease a 10-inch springform pan and line it with parchment.

2. Sift the cake flour and the cocoa powder together in a large bowl.

3. In the bowl of an electric mixer with the whip attachment, whisk together the egg yolks and ½ cup plus 1 tablespoon of the sugar until light and fluffy.

4. Stream in the oil, then the water and the vanilla extract.

5. Turn off the mixer, add the flour, cocoa, baking powder, and salt, and mix on low speed until moistened. Turn the mixer to high and whip for 30 seconds.

6. In a clean, dry bowl, whip the egg whites until foamy. Add 1 cup plus 1 tablespoon of sugar, 2 tablespoons at a time, and whip to stiff peaks.

7. Gently fold the egg whites into the chocolate mixture, pour into the prepared pan, and bake for 45 minutes to 1 hour, or until a toothpick inserted comes out clean or with dry crumbs.

8. Cool in the pan on a wire rack for 15 minutes, then turn out and cool completely.

9. With a serrated knife, level the top of the cake by slicing off any part that makes a dome, and set aside these excess pieces. Slice the cake into three layers.

10. Drop one layer into the bottom of the springform pan. Set a second layer aside.

11. Break up the third layer and the remains of the top that was sliced off. Distribute these evenly on a baking sheet. Dry them in the oven on the lowest possible heat for 15 to 20 minutes.

12. Grind the dried cake in a food processor to a fine crumb.

MOUSSE

4 ounces dark chocolate

½ cup heavy cream

4 eggs, separated

2 tablespoons granulated sugar

2 cups Ganache (see page 205), for topping

1. Place the chocolate in a large bowl. Fill a small saucepot with 2 inches of water and bring to a boil. Once the water has boiled, turn off the heat and place the bowl of chocolate on top of the pot of water. Stir occasionally until chocolate is completely melted.

2. In a medium-sized bowl, whip the cream until soft peaks form. Set aside.

3. In the clean, dry bowl of an electric mixer, whip the egg whites on medium speed until foamy. Slowly sprinkle in the sugar and whip on high until soft peaks form. Set aside.

4. Remove the chocolate bowl from the double boiler and wipe the bottom with a towel to dry (chocolate does not mix with water; it will seize and form an unusable ball). Quickly whisk in the egg yolks and whip until smooth and lightened in color.

5. Using a rubber spatula, gently fold the whipped cream into the chocolate mixture until 70 percent incorporated.

6. Gently fold the egg whites into the chocolate mixture until just incorporated.

7. Pour over the cake layer in the springform pan, top with the remaining cake layer, wrap in plastic wrap, and freeze overnight.

8. Remove the cake from the freezer and allow to sit at room temperature for 10 minutes. Run a hot knife around the inside of the pan; release the hinge, and remove the sides. Invert the cake onto a plate and carefully remove the pan bottom.

9. Pour the ganache while it is still warm over the top of the cake, allowing it to drip down the sides. Refrigerate for 10 minutes, or until the ganache is set.

10. Gently press cake crumbs to the side of the cake, being sure to cover any exposed mousse.

11. Refrigerate until ready to serve. Cut with a clean, hot knife.

MARTHA WASHINGTON'S GREAT CAKE

MAKES 1 (10-INCH) RING

"Great Cake" is one of Lady Martha Washington's most famous recipes. She wrote that she served it for her Twelfth Night party. The Twelfth Night of Christmas was the most celebrated holiday in the colonial era. Christmas Day was usually a more humble day spent at church and with family around a special meal, but eleven days later, fanciful balls and parties were thrown to mark the last day of the season.

Many people also used the holiday season for their wedding day because family and friends were already gathered. George and Martha Washington were wed on January 6, 1759—Twelfth Night. She served this "great" cake on her anniversary for guests who would assemble at Mount Vernon to celebrate.

Hannah Glasse has a similar recipe for a "rich" cake in her cookbook. This type of cake was reserved for the most special holidays to show off to guests. Although it is not the towering, colorful display that we think of when wedding cakes come to mind, it was indeed a showy pièce de résistance on the sweet table. These festive cakes were recognized as being luxurious because of their rare and expensive ingredients, not their exterior decoration. These cakes would be both rich and great because of the eggs and butter and sugar, candied fruit, costly imported spices including mace and nutmeg, and brandy and sherry.

Martha Washington's original recipe calls for an abundance of ingredients:

> Take 40 eggs and divide the whites from the yolks and beat them to a froth. Then work 4 pounds of butter to a cream and put the whites of eggs to it a Spoon full at a time till it is well work'd. Then put 4 pounds of sugar finely powdered to it in the same manner then put in the Yolks of eggs and 5 pounds of flour and 5 pounds of fruit. 2 hours will bake it. Add to it half an ounce of mace and nutmeg half a pint of wine and some fresh brandy.

She calls for five pounds of fruit. This recipe recommends combining a variety of candied fruits, but in the spirit of our founding mothers, feel free to get creative and use the fruits you prefer. Or, do as most eighteenth-century cooks did and use what is on hand in the cupboard. A particularly delicious combination in the winter is candied ginger with dried cranberries and candied orange peel. In the spring, dried apricots with candied lemon and dates make a superb substitution. No matter what the combination, the cake is sure to be *great*.

1½ cups dried black currants

⅓ cup candied orange peel, chopped

⅓ cup candied lemon peel, chopped

⅓ cup candied citron, chopped

¾ cup Madeira, divided

½ cup French brandy

3 cups all-purpose flour, sifted, divided

¾ cup (1½ sticks) unsalted butter, softened

1½ cups granulated sugar

3 large eggs, separated

½ teaspoon ground nutmeg

½ teaspoon ground mace

½ cup slivered almonds

1. Combine the dried and candied fruits in a medium-small bowl with ½ cup of the Madeira and ½ cup brandy. Cover with plastic wrap and refrigerate for at least 3 hours or overnight.

2. Preheat the oven to 325°F. Grease and flour a 10-inch tube pan.

3. Set a strainer over a small bowl and drain the fruits, reserving the liquid.

4. Toss ¼ cup flour with the fruits to coat.

5. In the bowl of an electric mixer with the paddle attachment, cream the butter with half of the sugar until it is light and fluffy. Scrape down the sides of the bowl, add the remaining sugar, and beat again.

6. In a small bowl, whisk the egg yolks until they are light and smooth, then add them to the butter and sugar. Beat for several minutes until light and fluffy, scraping down the sides of the bowl occasionally.

7. Sift together the remaining flour with the nutmeg and mace, then add it to the butter mixture, ½ cup at a time, alternately with the remaining ¼ cup of Madeira and the Madeira and brandy that the fruit soaked in, beating until smooth.

8. In a clean, dry bowl, whip the egg whites until firm peaks form.

9. By hand, gently fold the whites into the butter mixture until combined. Fold in the fruits and almonds in the same fashion.

10. Pour the batter into the prepared pan, smoothing the top with a spoon or spatula.

11. Bake for approximately 1½ hours, or until a toothpick inserted comes out clean. Cool the cake in the pan on a wire rack for 20 minutes before turning out onto a plate to cool completely.

12. Dust with confectioners' sugar or ice with sugar icing.

SUGAR ICING

3 large egg whites, at room temperature

1½ cups granulated sugar

Rose water or orange blossom water, to taste

1. In the clean, dry bowl of an electric mixer, begin beating the egg whites on medium speed until foamy. Turn the mixer to medium-high and add the sugar, 2 tablespoons at a time.

2. After a few minutes, or when soft peaks just begin to form, turn to high speed, continuing to add 2 tablespoons of sugar at a time.

3. Whip until all the sugar is incorporated. When medium-soft peaks form, add the rose water and continue whipping until stiff peaks form. Use immediately.

CHAPTER 3

Cobblers & Crisps

THE MOST PRACTICAL EIGHTEENTH-CENTURY DESSERTS WERE THOSE THAT RELIED ON FRESH SEASONAL INGREDIENTS OR ON PRESERVED FOODSTUFFS REQUIRING LITTLE PREPARATION. EVEN WITHOUT A RELIABLE OVEN, THE VERY EARLY SETTLERS COULD MAKE COBBLERS IN A CAST IRON DUTCH OVEN BY PLACING EITHER SWEET OR SAVORY INGREDIENTS IN THE BOTTOM AND LAYING SOME FORM OF CRUST ON TOP.

Covered, the filling would stew and bubble in its own juices while the crust puffed and dried. For the first colonists facing extreme conditions, this was a method of stretching fruit, vegetables, or even game meat into a full meal that could serve many. Several British desserts akin to America's cobbler remain popular, including the slump, grunt, and pandowdy.

Eventually, as more settlers came to America and conditions improved, cobblers and crisps were inspired by German food traditions. Cooks began baking cobblers and crisps rather than boiling them, covered, over a fire, resulting in a finer, tastier crust. French settlers introduced butter into the cobbler or crisp or pie dough, replacing the original suet and refining the dessert into a tastier, flakier confection.

Nearly any kind of fruit, fresh, cooked, or preserved, was and still is suitable for these desserts. Baked in pans or individual dishes, the sweetened fruit becomes comfortingly soft and juicy, while the cloak of butter, flour, sugar, spices, oats, and nuts transforms into a crisp complementary topping.

This type of dessert is humbler than some of the more elaborate or structural pieces in the book. It would probably have been reserved for more modest family meals or sweet tables for intimate guests. However, since sugar, and anything sweetened with it, was so popular and was increasingly becoming a part of the common diet, some form of dessert was almost always expected at the end of a meal.

OAT AND NUT STREUSEL

MAKES APPROXIMATELY 4 CUPS

This German-inspired topping is the perfect complement to baked fruit-based desserts and coffeecakes. Many German immigrants arrived early in the colonies. Some were from sects that left their homeland seeking religious freedom with William Penn's new promise of tolerance. As the German Amish and Mennonites settled farmland in the new territory, they were mistakenly referred to as Pennsylvania Dutch. While the name is incorrect, it remains lovingly attached to their baking traditions today.

This mixture of sugar, flour, and spices is excellent when combined with regional nuts, or the favorite of the cook. Pecans lend a sweet note to the dessert, while walnuts add crunch, and macadamia nuts impart a rich flavor. America's founding cooks would have used what they had in the cupboard or what was being harvested near them. Any combination of nuts works well.

6 ounces (1½ sticks) unsalted butter

1 cup granulated sugar

¾ cup brown sugar

1 teaspoon salt

1½ cups all-purpose flour

1 tablespoon cinnamon

1 teaspoon ground nutmeg

¾ cup rolled oats

1½ cups chopped nuts

1. In the bowl of an electric mixer fitted with the paddle attachment, on low speed, mix the butter, sugars, and salt until only pea-sized bits of butter remain.

2. Add the flour, cinnamon, nutmeg, and oats and mix a few turns.

3. Add the nuts and continue mixing on low speed until the flour is absorbed; it should be crumbly looking.

CHEF'S NOTE

This topping freezes very well. To freeze, spread on a sheet pan or cookie sheet in the freezer. Once frozen, keep in a bag in the freezer.

Pear and Sour Cherry Cobbler

In the eighteenth century, cherries were frequently preserved, made into wine, dried, and used in baked goods. The puddings (baked or boiled in pastry) and cherry pies that were also common inspired this cobbler, which marries tart fruit with a crisp German streusel.

Dried and candied fruit were available in various shops, but cookbooks of the period offered recipes for women who wished to engage in the lengthy task of drying fruit themselves. In *The Art of Cookery Made Plain and Easy,* Hannah Glasse included a recipe:

How to dry cherries

Take eight pounds of cherries, one pound of the beſt confectioners' ſugar, ſtone the cherries over a great deep baſon or glaſs, and lay them one by one in rows, and ſtrew a little ſugar: thus do till your baſon is full to the top, and let them ſtand till next day; then pour them out into a great poſnet, ſet them on the fire, let them boil very faſt a quarter of an hour, or more; then pour them again into your baſon, and let them ſtand two or three days; then take them out, lay them one by one on hair-ſieves, and ſet them in the ſun, or an oven, till they are dry, turning them every day upon dry ſieves; if in the oven, it muſt be as little warm as you can juſt feel it, when you hold your hand in it.

1½ cups dried sweet cherries

½ cup brandy

8 Bartlett pears, peeled, cored, and sliced

1 cup granulated sugar

2 tablespoons cornstarch

1 teaspoon orange zest

1 tablespoon ground clove

1 recipe (about 4 cups) Oat and Nut Streusel (see page 52)

1. In a small bowl, combine the cherries and brandy and refrigerate for at least 2 hours or overnight.

2. Preheat the oven to 375°F. Grease eight 1-cup ramekins or a 9 × 13-inch baking dish.

3. Toss all the ingredients except the streusel together in a large bowl, spoon into the ramekins or baking dish, top with streusel, and bake for approximately 20 minutes or until the topping is brown and the filling is bubbling.

4. Serve warm and/or with vanilla ice cream.

APPLE AND FIG CRUMBLE

MAKES 8 SERVINGS

The Spanish introduced figs to the Americas in the early 1500s, and they have thrived on these shores for five hundred years. Throughout the eighteenth century Americans purchased imported figs and grew them locally as the climate permitted. Naturally, the Mediterranean fruits thrived in the warmer climes of the southern colonies: the Carolinas, Georgia, Virginia. George Washington, in fact, is known to have had a fondness for the fruit. Records show that in 1772 he sent an order to the West Indies for "a Pot of good dryed Figs" and desired them only if they were reasonably priced. By 1797 he was growing the fruit at Mount Vernon as well, possibly for enjoying them both fresh and in dried foods used in the Christmas table setting. Many estate owners grew what were considered exotic or tropical fruits to supply their kitchens with produce. Nothing would impress a guest more than biting into pineapple, oranges, and figs tucked into a sweet ending to a meal.

This richly flavored crumble relies not only on the concentrated sweetness of dried figs, but also on the intense flavor achieved by precooking the fruit with Madeira, sugar, cinnamon, and vanilla, ingredients that were popular in the eighteenth century as well.

1 bottle (750 ml) Madeira wine

1½ cups granulated sugar

15 dried figs, stemmed and cubed

3 sticks cinnamon

1 vanilla bean, split lengthwise

8 Granny Smith apples, peeled, cored, and sliced

1 recipe (about 4 cups) Oat and Nut Streusel (see page 52)

Whipped cream or ice cream, for serving

1. Preheat the oven to 350°F. Grease eight 1-cup ramekins or a 9 × 13-inch baking dish with butter.

2. In a medium saucepan, bring the Madeira, sugar, figs, cinnamon sticks, and vanilla bean to a boil. Reduce the heat to medium and cook for 20 to 30 minutes, or until thickened and reduced by half.

3. Place the apples in a medium-sized ovenproof bowl. Remove the saucepan from the heat and pour the mixture over the apples. Stir the mixture until we combined. Discard the vanilla bean and cinnamon stick.

4. Evenly divide the mixture among the prepared ramekins (or place in the baking dish).

5. Top each ramekin with ½ cup of the streusel (or spread all of the topping over the baking dish).

6. Place the ramekins (or baking dish) on a baking pan. Bake for 25 to 30 minutes, or until the tops are golden brown and the filling begins to bubble.

7. Serve warm with whipped cream or vanilla ice cream.

APPLE CRANBERRY COBBLER

MAKES 6 SERVINGS

Colonial Americans found native cranberries similar in flavor to the lingonberries with which they had been familiar in Europe, although they quickly learned the cranberry required quite a bit of sweetening.

Benjamin Franklin so loved the bitter little berries that he wrote to his wife, Deborah, requesting her to ship several barrels to him in England and in France. He replied after receiving one such shipment in 1770, "Thanks for the Cranberrys. I am as ever Your affectionate Husband B Franklin."

Franklin most likely did not eat his cranberries as they were. He would have enjoyed them baked into a treat. In 1782 his friend Jonathan Williams Jr. went one step further and offered up the finished product: "I have lately received some Cranberrys from Boston. . . . I will pick out enough to make you a few Cranberry Tarts."

In the eighteenth century, berries were most often preserved or stewed to sweeten them for use in pies. This process also helped to make berries keep longer in larders or springhouses, before refrigerators kept them chilly.

This cobbler relies upon the apples and the oat topping to add sweetness to the cranberries and to create a light dessert that is pleasantly tart. It is an updated version of the sort that appeared in late-eighteenth-century cookbooks from people like Amelia Simmons. Her recipe for cranberry tart called for "Cranberries. Stewed, strained, and sweetened, put in paste No. 9 [a sweet, butter pastry], add spices till grateful, and baked gently."

2 cups apple cider, divided
⅛ cup granulated sugar
¼ cup brown sugar, packed
Pinch of kosher salt
3 tablespoons plus ½ teaspoon cornstarch
1½ teaspoons ground cinnamon
¾ cups fresh cranberries
4 Granny Smith apples, peeled, cored, and sliced
1 recipe (about 4 cups) Oat and Nut Streusel (see page 52)

1. In a medium-sized saucepan, combine 1½ cups of the cider, the two sugars, and the salt and bring to a boil. Grease six 1-cup ramekins, or a 9 × 13-inch baking dish.

2. In a small bowl, whisk together the cornstarch and cinnamon, then make a slurry by whisking the remaining ½ cup of cider into the cornstarch and cinnamon.

3. When the cider and sugars come to a boil, whisk in the slurry and return to a boil, stirring continuously. Set aside.

4. Preheat the oven to 375°F.

5. Place the apples and cranberries in a large bowl, pour the hot cider mixture over them, and toss. Spoon into the ramekins or baking dish, top with streusel, and bake for approximately 20 minutes or until the topping is brown and the filling is bubbling.

6. Serve warm with vanilla ice cream.

PEACH AND RASPBERRY COBBLER

MAKES 8 SERVINGS

This is the most traditional cobbler recipe in the book, because the method goes back to the very first settlers in the country, who did not yet have brick beehive ovens and sometimes endured living in small huts while building more permanent structures. It's also more akin to what southerners still consider a cobbler with its biscuitlike topping. While delicious with peaches and raspberries, try it with any variation of fruits that are in season.

BISCUIT TOPPING

4½ cups all-purpose flour

1 tablespoon salt

¼ cup sugar

3 tablespoons baking powder

8 ounces (2 sticks) unsalted butter, cubed

1¾ cups whole milk

FRUIT FILLING

½ cup granulated sugar

⅓ cup sour cream

1 large egg

2 tablespoons all-purpose flour

1 teaspoon vanilla extract

5 ripe peaches, sliced, skins intact

1 pint fresh raspberries

1. Preheat the oven to 350°F. Grease a 2-quart baking dish.

2. Prepare the biscuit topping: In the bowl of an electric mixer with the paddle attachment, place the flour, salt, sugar, and baking powder, and mix to combine.

3. Add the cubed butter and mix on low speed until the butter is broken into pea-sized pieces and the mixture resembles wet sand.

4. Stream in the milk and mix until just combined. Set the dough aside.

5. Prepare the fruit filling: In a medium-sized bowl, whisk together the sugar, sour cream, egg, flour, and vanilla.

6. Add the peaches and raspberries to the cream mixture and toss to coat. Spoon into the baking dish, drop large tablespoons of biscuit dough onto the filling, and bake for 15 to 20 minutes or until the biscuits are browned and the filling bubbling.

RHUBARB AND STRAWBERRY COBBLER

MAKES 6 SERVINGS

Rhubarb was introduced to Maine at the end of the eighteenth century. This was an era when plants were quickly spreading from their native lands as travelers brought home seeds from voyages abroad or sent them to friends in the fledgling nation. The first U.S. horticulturists, such as Philadelphia's John Bartram, collected, cataloged, and propagated seeds to introduce new species.

Rhubarb quickly spread to other northern colonies and flourished in Massachusetts, where it grew well in the cold climate and was a welcome first crop in spring. It became known as the "pie plant" for its use with sweet berries in desserts.

When preparing fruit pies, eighteenth-century bakers not only created flavorful combinations like this classic pairing of tart rhubarb and sweet strawberries, but also focused on making high-quality pastry toppings.

1½ pounds fresh rhubarb, washed, leaves removed, and diced (or frozen rhubarb, thawed)

2 cups large fresh strawberries, stemmed and halved

1 teaspoon lemon juice

2 tablespoons water (if using frozen rhubarb, omit water)

¼ cup granulated sugar

¼ cup brown sugar, packed

½ teaspoon lemon zest

½ teaspoon ground cinnamon

1 tablespoon plus 1 teaspoon cornstarch

1 recipe (about 4 cups) Oat and Nut Streusel (see page 52)

1. Preheat the oven to 350°F. Grease six 1-cup ramekins or one 9 × 9-inch baking dish.

2. In a large bowl toss together the rhubarb, strawberries, lemon juice, and water.

3. In a small bowl stir together the sugars, zest, cinnamon, and cornstarch.

4. Toss the sugar mixture with the fruit mixture. Spoon into the ramekins or baking dish and top with the streusel. Bake for approximately 20 minutes or until the streusel is browned and the filling is bubbling.

CHAPTER 4

Pies & Tarts

PIES OF THIS ERA WERE NO LESS VARIED, IF NOT MORE, THAN THOSE OF TODAY.
DOUGH WAS FASTER TO MAKE THAN BREAD, AND IT ADDED ADDITIONAL
NUTRITION TO ANY FILLING—LOBSTER, VENISON, RABBIT, BERRIES, OR APPLES.

Some pies were elegant and expensive, prepared with puff pastry and imported spices and citrus, while others were modest and frugal, consisting of a short dough and custard. Pies and tarts—cookbook authors interchanged the terms—were sweet or savory; they were filled with fresh fruit, dried fruit, meat, seafood, preserves, custards, or puddings. They had top crusts, bottom crusts, or both. They were prepared in deep dishes or shallow tins, and they were baked in ovens as well as in bake kettles (lidded pans that stood in hot coals in the fireplace, covered with additional embers).

One of the a few common attributes of all the "pyes" and "tarts" is that a dough and a filling were combined and baked in a pan. Eighteenth-century cookbook authors included numerous recipes for pies and tarts in their books, a testament to the significance of these dishes. Most authors of the period wrote in great detail about the preparation of "pastes" as well as individual pies and tarts.

Elizabeth Raffald, however, was fairly succinct in her suggestions, which served as an informative overview of the subject:

Raiſed Pies ſhould have a quick Oven, and well cloſed up, or your Pye will fall in the ſides. It ſhould have no Water put in, 'till the minute it goes to the Oven, it makes the Cruſt ſad, and is a great Hazard of the Pye running.—Light Paſte requires a moderate Oven, but not too ſlow, it will make them ſad, and a quick Oven will catch and burn it, and not give it Time to riſe; Tarts that are iced, require a ſlow Oven or the Iceing will be brown, and the Paſte not be near baked. Theſe Sort of Tarts ought to be made of Sugar Paſte, and rolled very thin.

PUMPKIN PIE

MAKES 1 (9-INCH) DEEP-DISH PIE

Although pumpkins were available in Britain, they have become synonymous with American foodways. Among the many squashes the Native Americans cultivated, the pumpkin is undoubtedly the most famous, due to the serving of pumpkin pie in 1623 at the Pilgrims' second Thanksgiving celebration. In fact, records reveal that early colonists in Connecticut postponed one of their Thanksgiving dinners because they couldn't obtain the molasses necessary for pie.

From the seventeenth century onward, Americans used pumpkin in numerous dishes besides pie. It is hardly surprising that the gourmet connoisseur Thomas Jefferson included a stylish soup recipe, complete with buttered croutons, in his collection of recipes.

This version of pumpkin pie is based on period recipes that, while quite pale, were flavorful and rich, due to the use of spices as well as eggs and cream.

1 recipe Pâte Brisée (see page 199)

¼ cup brown sugar

1 cup plus 3 tablespoons granulated sugar

1 teaspoon ground cinnamon

½ teaspoon freshly grated nutmeg

½ teaspoon ground allspice

1 teaspoon ground ginger

¼ teaspoon ground cloves

½ teaspoon salt

4 eggs

5¼ ounces pumpkin puree

¾ cup half-and-half

1. Preheat the oven to 325°F.

2. Roll the dough into a 10-inch circle ¼ inch thick. Fit it into a 9-inch pie tin, trim the excess, and crimp the edge. Refrigerate until ready to use.

3. Whisk together the sugars, spices, and salt, then whisk in the eggs until completely combined.

4. Whisk in the pumpkin, then the half-and-half.

5. Pour the custard into the pie shell and bake in the center of the oven until the crust is golden, the outer edge of the custard has puffed slightly, and the center is somewhat shiny and wobbles ever so slightly, approximately 25 to 30 minutes.

6. Cool on a rack to room temperature; refrigerate until cold before cutting.

THADDEUS KOSCIUSZKO TART

MAKES 1 (10-INCH) TART

This strawberry hazelnut tart is named for an unsung American hero, the general who emigrated from Poland to America to help the revolutionary cause. Thaddeus (Tadeusz) Kosciuszko showed up on Benjamin Franklin's doorstep in Philadelphia and volunteered to lead the troops. In 1776 the Continental Congress commissioned him Colonel of Engineers, and he fortified America's forts and rivers against the British navy and designed West Point.

Kosciuszko returned to Poland inspired by America's victory and led a battle of insurrection in 1794 against the surrounding European powers. When his forces lost, Catherine the Great imprisoned him for years. Kosciuszko returned to America and moved to Philadelphia, where his house remains a national landmark. He fought these battles because of his intense belief in equality and freedom. As a parting gift to America, when Kosciuszko left for the last time, he decreed that the money from his estate be used to buy freedom for slaves, help to educate them, and provide them with enough land to support themselves.

This dish is made as a tribute to the great general, engineer, and freedom fighter because he wrote that he loved strawberries, a fruit that grew wild and abundant in his "second home," America. This recipe calls for strawberry jam rather than fresh berries. Colonial cooks made jams to preserve berries for much longer than the fleeting growing season. Fresh berries bleed their natural juices and tend to make the crust soggy, so using jam leads to a chewy inside with a crunchy, flaky crust. Thaddeus also wrote that he loved drinking coffee, so we recommend that you enjoy this tart with a cup of brew.

10 ounces (2½ sticks) unsalted butter

8 ounces granulated sugar

½ teaspoon salt

1 egg

2 egg yolks

Splash of vanilla extract

2¼ cups all-purpose flour

1 teaspoon ground cinnamon

½ teaspoon ground cloves

¾ cup ground hazelnuts, toasted and cooled

10 ounces Strawberry Jam (see page 215, or store bought)

Egg wash

1. In the bowl of an electric mixer with the paddle attachment, beat together the butter, sugar, and salt until light and fluffy, scraping down the sides of the bowl and paddle often.

2. With the mixer running, add the egg and yolks one at a time, scraping down after each addition. Add the vanilla extract and beat until thoroughly combined.

3. Add the flour and spices, pulse the mixer until 50 percent incorporated, then add the hazelnuts and mix until fully combined.

4. Wrap the dough in plastic wrap and refrigerate for at least 2 hours or overnight.

5. Preheat the oven to 350°F.

6. Roll out half of the dough to ¼-inch thickness and fit into a 10-inch tart pan.

7. Spread the jam in an even layer over the dough.

8. Roll out the other half of the dough to ¼-inch thickness and cut it into twelve 1-inch-wide strips. Weave a six-by-six-strip lattice over the jam.

9. Refrigerate for 30 minutes before baking.

10. Paint with the egg wash and bake for 40 minutes, or until golden brown and flaky.

"Cannot Tell a Lie" Cherry Pie

MAKES 1 (9-INCH) PIE; SERVES 8

George Washington is famous for his love of cherries, because of the fable of the cherry tree he cut down as a boy. The story goes that when Washington was a six-year-old, he was given a hatchet and he amused himself with it in the garden by chopping pea splints and eventually by removing the bark from his father's favorite cherry tree. When the tree died and his father angrily asked who killed it, Washington remarked, "I cannot tell a lie. I killed the tree."

While this anecdote is useful in instructing children, it is not true. The cherry tree fable was made up by Parson Mason Weems in his biography of George Washington, written shortly after Washington's death. Little is known about Washington's childhood, so Weems took creative license in inventing stories to illustrate his heroic qualities. Today the parable persists.

The truth, though, is that Washington did grow cherries. He saw to it that many varieties flourished on the estate of Mount Vernon, including morello, which Hannah Glasse recommended in her recipe for cherry pie. We recommend a much more convenient and modern approach, using canned cherries. Purchase the highest quality cherry filling available for the best results.

1 double recipe (two 9-inch rounds) Pâte Brisée (see page 199)

5 cups red tart cherries, in juice

¾ cup granulated sugar

1 vanilla bean, split and scraped

4 tablespoons cornstarch

2½ tablespoons Kirchwasser

2½ tablespoons water

1 egg, whisked, for brushing

1. Preheat oven to 375°F.

2. Drain cherries in a strainer lined with cheesecloth or a tea towel. Wrap cherries in cloth and squeeze all remaining juice out. Reserve ½ cup juice.

3. Roll out half of the pie dough into an 11-inch circle and fit it into the pie tin. Trim the excess, prick the shell several times in different places with a fork to make small holes to allow it to ventilate, and refrigerate.

4. Roll the other half of the dough into a 10-inch circle and cut 1-inch strips from it, lay them on a baking sheet and place them in the refrigerator.

5. Place sugar, vanilla bean, cornstarch, ½ cup cherry liquid, and Kirchwasser in a medium-sized bowl and whisk to combine.

6. Add the cherries to the bowl and toss to coat. Transfer the cherries to the unbaked pie shell and brush the edge of the crust with egg.

7. Evenly space the pie dough strips across the top of the pie in two directions, giving a lattice effect, and trim the excess. Once complete brush the top with the remaining egg.

8. Place the pie on a baking sheet (to catch any spills in the oven) and bake for 20 to 30 minutes, or until the filling bubbles and the crust is golden brown.

9. Cool to room temperature before serving.

MACADAMIA AND COCONUT TART

MAKES 8 TARTLETS OR 1 (10-INCH) TART

Fortunate families who lived in port cities such as Charleston, Philadelphia, or Boston would have first pick of the produce in shops that benefited from the trade triangle. Exotic fruits including pineapple, coconut, mangoes, and bananas were available for purchase.

Wealthy families also had cooks who came to North America on the same trade routes. Those house servants native to the West Indies would have expertly dissected the fruits of their homeland to get the most out of them, including the coconut water and meat. This is a delicious and beautiful tart that would have impressed any city dweller's country cousins with its exotic combination of tropical ingredients.

CHOCOLATE SHORT CRUST

4 ounces (1 stick) unsalted butter, cubed and softened

½ cup granulated sugar

½ cup sifted all-purpose flour

1 cup unsweetened Dutch cocoa powder, sifted

¼ teaspoon salt

1 large egg

1 large egg yolk

FILLING

1¼ cups whole milk

2 large eggs

3 tablespoons granulated sugar

1 cup freshly grated unsweetened coconut flakes, lightly toasted

1 cup macadamia nuts, toasted and chopped

1. Prepare the chocolate short crust: In the bowl of an electric mixer on medium-high speed, cream the butter and sugar together until light and fluffy.

2. In a separate bowl, combine the flour, cocoa, and salt; stir to mix.

3. With the electric mixer on low, slowly add the dry ingredients to the butter and sugar mixture and beat just until combined. Add the egg and yolk and continue mixing until the dough just begins to hold together. Shape it into a flat round, about 5 inches in diameter. Wrap the dough in plastic and chill in the refrigerator for at least 1 hour before using.

4. Meanwhile, preheat the oven to 400°F. Grease a 10-inch tart pan or eight individual tart pans with butter, and coat lightly with flour.

5. Prepare the filling: In a medium bowl, whisk together the milk, eggs, and sugar until well combined. Set aside.

6. Remove the dough from the refrigerator and divide it into eight pieces if making small tarts, or leave as one piece if making one large tart as shown. Roll out each piece into a circle 2 inches wider than the tart pans.

Place the rounds in the greased and floured pans and trim the dough to fit.

7. Place the tartlet shells or 10-inch shell on a large baking sheet. Line each unbaked shell with a piece of parchment or wax paper cut 3 inches longer than the tart pan and fill with dried beans or pie weights. Bake for 8 to 10 minutes for the smaller tarts or 10 to 15 minutes for the large one. Remove the foil and bake for 5 minutes more, or until the dough is firm and set to the touch but not browned. Remove the shells and reduce the oven temperature to 350°F.

8. Sprinkle each tart shell with the coconut and nuts. Carefully pour the filling into the shells.

9. Gently transfer the tartlets on their baking sheet to the oven. Bake for 10 to 15 minutes for individual tarts or 15 to 20 minutes for the large tart until the custard is set and a knife inserted near the center comes out clean.

10. Cool to room temperature on a wire rack. Refrigerate for at least 2 hours before serving.

JOHNNY APPLESEED'S PIE

MAKES 1 (9-INCH) PIE

The person behind this fable was an eccentric man who roamed the frontier in rags, barefoot, and with a pot for a hat. He roped canoes together to float down the river with seeds and gave away his crops. The real Johnny Appleseed was by all accounts as odd as the songs describe. John Chapman was born in 1775 and eventually became the stuff of folklore when in 1801 he set out down the Ohio River to propagate apple orchards.

He walked across 100,000 square miles of Midwestern wilderness and prairie, acquired more than 1,000 acres of farmland to create orchards and nurseries, and made peace with Native Americans and western settlers alike. While he is a champion to many, some agriculture purists blame Chapman for beginning the American custom of growing only one species of a plant, rather than embracing many varieties. This, they say, led to today's somewhat bland and uniform fruit.

There is also debate over whether Johnny's apples were used to make pies or cider. Rather than brewing beer with hops and other hard-to-find ingredients on the plains, many pressed apples into cider and left it overnight to bubble into a low-alcohol alternative to ales. "Hard" cider left to ferment kept many traders and frontiersmen warm at night. New Englanders, too, imbibed hard cider. John Adams regularly wrote that he began his day with a cup of cider before breakfast. The American tradition of cider making continued well into the what modern day and was an especially popular skill during Prohibition when making or selling alcoholic beverages was illegal.

No matter what John Chapman's intent was in spreading apples, he is famous still for his work in horticulture and will forever be synonymous with this distinctly American fruit. In fact, Fort Wayne, Indiana, has a festival in his honor near the Johnny Appleseed Gravesite, and to this day the town celebrates his eccentric character and, of course, his signature crop. This classic pie is in his honor, and that of all American folk heroes who changed the culinary landscape of America in its early years.

5 Granny Smith apples, peeled, cored, and sliced

¼ cup granulated sugar

¼ cup brown sugar

1 teaspoon ground cinnamon

2 tablespoons soft butter

2 tablespoons all-purpose flour

2 recipes Pâte Brisée (see page 199)

1. Preheat the oven to 375°F.

2. In a large bowl toss together the apples, sugars, and cinnamon. Add the butter in small pieces and the flour, toss again, and set aside.

3. Divide the pie dough in half. On a lightly floured surface, roll out each dough ball into a 11-inch circle approximately ¼ inch thick.

4. Ease one circle into a 9-inch pie tin, fill with the apple mixture, and place the second circle on top.

5. Trim the pastry to within ½ inch of the pie plate, tuck the edges under, and crimp with the fingers or press with a fork.

6. Using a sharp knife, cut several slits in the top crust to vent.

7. Bake 30 to 40 minutes, or until the top turns golden brown and the filling starts to bubble.

8. Cool on a wire rack for 5 to 10 minutes. Serve warm.

Fig and Anise Tart

MAKES 1 (10-INCH) TART

From professional pâtissiers to wealthy wives to domestic servants, men and women alike understood that the ability to prepare tasty, tender pastry was a necessary skill. Whether in the kitchen at home or at school, a girl would learn to combine ingredients, roll the dough, and create sweet or savory pastries to perfection. This was an art developed with pride.

Topping a well-made crust with exotic flavors would always impress callers. Imagine the delight of a beau when his lady of interest presented this tart to finish a meal. It would have been an indication of quite the dowry to come, with its expensive use of ingredients. This recipe combines anise, a Chinese spice imported from Asia, and figs, the fruit of the Greek gods, with their fickle growing season and sensuous shape.

FILLING

1 vanilla bean, pod reserved for glaze
8 ounces (2 sticks) unsalted butter
½ cup sugar
½ teaspoon cinnamon
2 teaspoons nutmeg
3 eggs
3 egg yolks
1 tablespoon anisette
¾ cup Apricot Preserves (see page 210)
½ 1 recipe Kosciuszko tart dough (see page 64), chilled for 30 minutes
1¼ cups sliced almonds, toasted
2 pints black Mission figs, stemmed and halved

GLAZE

4 tablespoons (½ stick) unsalted butter
1 tablespoon honey
Zest of 1 orange
1 teaspoon lemon zest
Pinch of salt
Vanilla bean pod

1. Preheat the oven to 350°F.

2. Prepare the filling: Using a paring knife, slice the vanilla bean in half lengthwise and scrape the seeds from the pod with the back of the knife.

3. In the bowl of an electric mixer fitted with the paddle attachment, on medium speed cream together the butter, sugar, vanilla seeds, cinnamon, and nutmeg. Scrape down the sides of the bowl often.

4. With the mixer running on low speed, add the eggs and yolks, one at a time, scraping down the sides of the bowl each after addition. Add the anisette and stir to combine.

5. Prepare the glaze: Place all ingredients in a small saucepan and heat, stirring constantly, over low heat until the butter is melted. Turn off the heat and leave the pan on the stove to keep warm.

6. Spread a thin layer of apricot preserves on the bottom of the tart shell. Sprinkle the almonds evenly over the apricot preserves layer.

7. Fill the tart shell three-quarters full with filling and spread it evenly.

8. Arrange the figs, skin side down, atop the filling.

9. Brush the figs with the warm glaze. Bake the tart for 30 minutes, or until the figs caramelize, the cream sets, and the tart shell is brown. Let cool for 1 hour before serving.

ORANGE LAVENDER CURD TART

MAKES 1 (10-INCH) TART

Lavender, rosemary, mint, roses, and chamomile were grown in kitchen gardens and used in recipes as much for their fragrance as for their flavor. Known as "strewing herbs," these plants were strewn upon the ground of dining halls to release a pleasant smell when walked upon by guests. Since the Middle Ages in Europe, these herbs masked odors, and people believed in their curative powers, especially for women in childbirth.

Lavender appears in countless dessert recipes, possibly because of the French inspiration popular in the American colonies. It is also used for medicines and "tonics," household cleaners, soaps, and beauty treatments.

½ recipe Pâte Sucrée (see page 200)

3 eggs

7 egg yolks

¾ cup granulated sugar

Zest of 1 orange

8 ounces freshly squeezed orange juice

8 ounces (2 sticks) butter, cubed

1 teaspoon dried lavender flowers

1. Preheat the oven to 350°F.

2. On a lightly floured surface, roll the pie dough into a 12-inch circle. Gently fit the dough into a greased tart pan and trim the excess.

3. Prick the dough with the tines of a fork all over. Freeze for 10 to 15 minutes.

4. Line the shell with parchment paper or greased foil and fill with pie weights. Bake for 8 to 10 minutes, or until the edges begin to brown.

5. Remove the liner and weights and return the shell to the oven to finish baking, another 8 to 10 minutes or until the entire crust is golden brown and flaky.

6. Cool the shell to room temperature while you prepare the filling.

7. In a stainless steel saucepot, whisk together the eggs, egg yolks, sugar, and orange zest until combined.

8. Whisk in the orange juice and cook over medium heat, stirring constantly, until the custard is very thick. When you drag a spatula through it, you should be able to see the bottom of the pot for a few seconds before the curd falls back on itself.

9. Remove from the heat, pour the curd into a large bowl, and whisk in the butter and lavender flowers.

10. Let stand, stirring occasionally, until the curd cools slightly.

11. Pour the curd into the tart shell, cover with plastic wrap, and chill until ready to serve.

CHEF'S NOTE

Low heat and constant stirring are imperative when making curd in order to prevent scrambling the eggs and/or burning the curd.

Summer Berry Tart

When making this tart, use the freshest berries available. This tart is best made in the summer when berries are in full bounty. Honeysuckle is also a summer treat that can be plucked from the vine. Just as in centuries past, shoppers in Philadelphia and other founding cities can walk the cobblestone paths of old farmers' markets to select the best produce. Now called Old Town Farmers' Market, the square in Alexandria, Virginia, was founded in 1753 and was where George Washington's slaves walked from their homes at Mount Vernon estate on Sunday afternoons to sell their crops and wares and socialize. Likewise, in 1745 sheds were built for merchants to sell their wares at Philadelphia's Head House Square, where shoppers still gather on weekends for local bounty.

½ recipe Pâte Sucrée (see page 200)

1 recipe Pastry Cream (see page 202), replacing vanilla extract with honeysuckle extract

1 pint raspberries, washed and dried

1 pint blueberries, washed and dried

1 pint blackberries, washed and dried

½ cup apricot jam

3–4 tablespoons water

1. Preheat the oven to 350°F.

2. On a lightly floured surface, roll the pie dough into a 12-inch circle. Gently fit the dough into a greased 10-inch tart pan and trim the excess.

3. Prick the dough with a fork in a few places to allow steam to vent from it. Place the entire pie shell in the freezer for 10 to 15 minutes to allow the butter to remain cold and solid, resulting in a flakier crust.

4. Line the shell with parchment paper or greased foil and fill with pie weights. Bake for 8 to 10 minutes, or until the edges begin to brown.

5. Remove the liner and weights and return the shell to the oven to finish baking, another 8 to 10 minutes or until the entire crust is golden brown and flaky.

6. Cool the shell to room temperature while you prepare the filling.

7. Fill the baked shell with the pastry cream and arrange the fruit on top.

8. In a small saucepan, heat the apricot jam with the water until it is warm and thinned.

9. Using a pastry brush, brush the apricot jam over the tart to seal the cream and gloss the fruit.

10. Chill until ready to serve.

Mrs. Goodfellow's Lemon Meringue Pie

MAKES 1 (9-INCH) PIE

Mrs. Goodfellow was a visionary in the food industry and a woman ahead of her time. In an era when women did not own businesses, she forged ahead with her bakery and school and catered parties for many wealthy socialites in the Philadelphia. She is credited with the invention of the lemon meringue pie, in addition to many spectacular recipes.

Her recipe for lemon custard uses only the yolks of eggs. At some time in her lessons, she must have had a stroke of frugality and whipped the whites with sugar instead of letting them go to waste. She put this meringue on top of the custard, let it brown in the dying heat of the oven, and voilà! Culinary history was made. This iconic, truly American confection is just as pretty as it is tasty.

3 large eggs

7 large egg yolks

1 cup granulated sugar, divided

Zest of 2 lemons

1 cup freshly squeezed lemon juice

8 ounces (2 sticks) cold unsalted butter, cubed

1 recipe Pâte Brisée (see page 199), in a 9-inch pie pan, baked and cooled

5 large egg whites

1. In a stainless steel saucepot, whisk together the eggs, egg yolks, ¾ cup of the sugar, and the lemon zest until combined.

2. Whisk in the lemon juice and cook over medium heat, stirring constantly, until the custard is very thick. When you drag a spatula through it, you should be able to see the bottom of the pot for a few seconds before the curd falls back on itself.

3. Remove from the heat, pour the curd into a large bowl, and whisk in the butter.

4. Let stand, stirring occasionally, until the curd cools slightly.

5. Pour the curd into the pie shell, cover with plastic wrap, and chill until the curd is cold.

6. Preheat the oven to 400°F.

7. In the clean, dry bowl of an electric mixer, whip the egg whites on medium speed until foamy. Sprinkle in the remaining ¼ cup of sugar, 1 tablespoon at a time, and whip on high speed until stiff, glossy peaks form.

8. Spoon or pipe the meringue over the cooled curd and bake until the meringue has browned, about 12 to 15 minutes.

9. Serve at room temperature.

CHEF'S NOTE

Low heat and constant stirring are imperative when making curd in order to prevent scrambling the eggs and/or burning the curd.

CHAPTER 5

Custards, Puddings & Fools

In *The Art of Cookery Made Plain and Easy* Hannah Glasse listed two recipes for "Indian Pudding" and one for cornmeal "Mush" in a chapter titled "Several New Receipts Adapted to the American Mode of Cooking."

Cooks may have used what they had on hand, but they were dedicated to creating the most beautiful desserts possible.

Eighteenth-century cooks did not have food coloring, but that did not stop them from adding extra color to whipped cream, syllabubs, gelatin, and custard. Hannah Glasse wrote that *"you may colour ſome with the juice of ſpinage, ſome with ſaffron, and ſome with cochineal (juſt as you fancy)."*

Cochineal is an insect that was imported from Central America, ground into powder, and used as red food coloring. A form of it is still used today. In fact, it's gotten a bit of bad press recently because vegetarians demanded it be removed from berry-flavored smoothies sold at national chain stores.

All ingredients were natural in the eighteenth century, not just food dye. Likewise, gelatin was extremely popular and impressive because of the work and expense involved. Up until the 1870s, cooks could not purchase ready-made gelatin. They had to make their own, using animal parts that naturally contain gelatin, including calves' feet, pigs' skin, isinglass, and even ivory shavings. The most elite chefs used isinglass, or *col de poisson*, as it was called in French kitchens. Isinglass could be purchased in powder form and was boiled down, strained, and further reduced. It was made from the dried and shredded swim bladders of sturgeon. It took much less work than scraping calves' feet and did not have a glue-like flavor or consistency. Chefs further took steps to clarify sugar before adding it to isinglass to result in a transparent and jewel-like gelatin that was not murky.

Happily, modern cooks can use simple powdered gelatin in place of hooves or fish parts. The recipes in this book call for unflavored gelatin. Just as the original recipes use fruit or wine to flavor gelatin, these adaptations get their pizzazz from natural additions.

BERRY GELÉE

MAKES 1½ CUPS

This gelatin makes a gorgeous dark-colored dessert. Serve it in champagne coupes for a presentation that was thoroughly modern in the late 1700s. The coupe, which was later replaced with the champagne flute, was especially popular in the era. Historic rumors abound that the coupe was hand blown as a faithful re-creation of Marie Antoinette's breast. But, like her infamous cake quote, it may not be true. Several French femme fatales share in this story—it is said that coupes are the replica of Empress Josephine and Madame de Pompadour, the mistress of Louis XV. There is some record of coupes being in existence as early as the 1660s, well before Marie Antoinette's reign. However, she did in fact commission several milk bowls modeled on her breasts. The bowls were kept at her "pleasure dairy," where the queen and other aristocrats dressed as milkmaids and frolicked in the fields of Versailles.

1 tablespoon unflavored gelatin
¼ cup cold water
¾ cup blueberry juice
½ cup raspberry juice
Granulated sugar, to taste, depending on sweetness of fruit juices

1. In a medium-sized bowl, sprinkle the gelatin over the cold water in a thin, even layer to soften for 10 minutes.

2. In a small saucepot bring the fruit juices and sugar to a boil.

3. Remove from the heat and pour over the softened gelatin. Stir to combine.

4. Portion into four glasses and refrigerate for at least 2 hours or until completely set.

CORN PUDDING WITH STRAWBERRY GELÉE

MAKES 6 SERVINGS

This dessert uses two uniquely American ingredients that are in season simultaneously. Before coming to America, most Europeans did not consider corn an edible crop. It was used as feed for cattle, pigs, and horses but not for human consumption. However, after a few hard winters, settlers' pragmatism changed all that when Europeans realized that Native Americans were harvesting corn crops and living from its sweet kernels. Early accounts of Native American food mention combining crushed corn with strawberries and molasses to make a sweetened dessert. This recipe is an accumulation of many inspirations going back to native ingredients found in America.

CORN PUDDING

1 cup corn kernels, fresh or frozen

2 cups whole milk

1 teaspoon salt

1 cup granulated sugar, divided

6 eggs

3 tablespoons unsalted butter

1. Prepare an ice bath (see note on next page).

2. In a medium-sized saucepot, simmer the corn, milk, salt, and ⅔ cup of the sugar over medium heat until the corn is tender. Carefully transfer the corn mixture to a blender, puree it, and return it to the pot. Alternatively, you can puree it with an immersion blender.

3. Whisk together the remaining ⅓ cup sugar and the eggs, then quickly whisk them into the warm corn mixture.

4. Return the pot to the stove and cook, stirring constantly, until the pudding is thick and grainy.

5. Transfer the mixture to a medium-sized bowl and whisk in the butter.

6. Set the pudding over the ice bath and stir regularly until it has cooled.

7. Portion out into six glasses, cover, and refrigerate for at least 1 hour.

STRAWBERRY GELÉE

1 tablespoon unflavored gelatin

1 cup water, divided

¾ cup granulated sugar

1½ cups fresh strawberries, chopped

1. In a metal bowl, sprinkle the gelatin over ¼ cup of cold water to bloom for 10 minutes.

2. In a saucepot smaller in diameter than the metal bowl, bring the sugar and ¾ cup of water to a boil. Turn off the heat, and place the bowl of gelatin on top to soften.

3. When the gelatin has liquefied, stir it into the sugar mixture. Pour one-sixth of the mixture (about ¼ cup) over the chilled corn pudding in each glass.

4. Drop ¼ cup of the chopped strawberries into each glass, and refrigerate until set, at least 1 hour.

CHEF'S NOTE: MAKING AN ICE BATH

Fill a large bowl with ice cubes and cold water, about halfway up the bowl. Insert a smaller, heatproof bowl into the large bowl. Arrange the ice cubes around the bowl. Pour whatever is to be chilled into the smaller bowl (or, if it is already in a bowl, nestle that into the ice) and stir occasionally to allow the heat to escape until the mixture has cooled.

Use of an ice bath is especially crucial for custards, ice cream bases, and the like. If a custard mixture is not iced, the eggs will continue to cook and then scramble, making the mixture unusable.

Mint Gelée

MAKES 2 CUPS

Mint jelly became all the rage in the 1960s and was generally served with lamb. Well before this steak-house classic, Americans were enjoying the slightly sweet herb in gelatin. Because all sorts of varieties of mint grow exceedingly well in the many climates throughout America, it was a mainstay of the garden ever since the early settlers arrived. In the eighteenth century, mint was used by physicians and housewives alike for its medicinal purposes. Colonists used mint in home remedies to cure colic, indigestion, toothaches, digestive odors, and even mad dog bites. Many enjoyed it in tea to help with insomnia, headaches, and heartburn—and because it was not taxed by the British but grew in the kitchen garden. One can imagine serving this mint gelée after a heavy meal to aid in the digestion of the feast and because it adds a delightful color to a sweet table with its natural dark green hues.

2 cups granulated sugar
2 cups water, divided
2 ounces fresh mint (stems and leaves)
1 tablespoon unflavored gelatin

1. In a small saucepot, bring the sugar and 1¾ cups of water to a boil. Turn off the heat, stir in the mint, and cover with a tea towel. Let rest for 20 minutes, or longer for a stronger flavor.

2. In a metal bowl wider than the saucepot, sprinkle the gelatin over ¼ cup of cold water to bloom for 10 minutes.

3. Reheat the sugar water just to a boil, turn off the heat, and place the gelatin bowl on top of the pot to soften.

4. When the gelatin has liquefied, stir it into the sugar mixture and pour the mixture into a gelatin mold or four pretty glasses.

5. Refrigerate until set, at least 1 hour.

CHAMPAGNE GELÉE

MAKES 4 SERVINGS

Champagne got its legacy as a drink of celebration and high class because it was served to celebrate the coronation of French kings. Since the eleventh century, royal coronations were held in the cathedral of Reims, the ancient capital city of the Champagne region. When bubbling wines were developed in the area in the seventeenth century, they were naturally served and became a status symbol. Champagne was a favorite at all the courts of Europe. Madame de Pompadour, mistress to Louis XV said, "The wine of Champagne is the only one that makes women beautiful after drinking." Of course, Americans took this regal beverage one step further.

This recipe has very few ingredients, so it's paramount to choose the highest quality available. The gelatin does not affect the flavor of the recipe, so be certain to use a sparkling wine that is delicious on its own. For dessert, choose a demi-sec, which is slightly sweet. However, for an interesting palate-cleansing course in the middle of a meal or to begin, try this recipe with no addition of sugar and use a very dry ultra brut.

1 tablespoon unflavored gelatin
1 cup cold champagne
1 cup water
1 cup granulated sugar

1. In a medium-sized bowl, sprinkle the gelatin over the champagne in a thin, even layer to soften for 10 minutes.

2. In a small saucepot bring the water and sugar to a boil.

3. Remove from the heat and pour over the champagne and softened gelatin; stir to combine.

4. Portion into four glasses and refrigerate for at least 2 hours or until completely set.

5. For a bubble effect, gently insert and remove toothpick or knife into the set gelatin a few times until lightly broken.

VANILLA BEAN BLANCMANGE

MAKES 10–12 SERVINGS

Blancmange, or blanc manger, dates at least to the fourteenth century in Europe. Translated as "white food," this term refers to the colorless, or white, foods that became stylish during the end of the Medieval Era in France and eventually in England as well. Early cookery books and manuscripts reference this dish prepared in many varieties, both savory and sweet, relying on such colorless ingredients as poultry, fish, sugar, cream, almonds, and eggs. In the fourteenth and fifteenth centuries, it was commonly served as the first course and included shredded chicken breast, rice, or ground almonds.

Blancmange evolved over the centuries into a sweet gelatin served for dessert. Eighteenth-century English cookbook authors commonly offered a number of recipes, all of which were essentially jellies prepared with isinglass (a form of gelatin), ground almonds, sugar, and very little cream. The gelatin would have been poured into an elaborate copper mold, chilled, and put on an elegant platter and placed in a prominent position on the sweet table to add height and structure.

One popular variation, breaking with the "white" tradition, in fact, called for spinach juice, which resulted in a green jelly. As with most desserts, it was rarely served on its own but was part of an elaborate display in the second or last course of a meal. Blancmange would have been accompanied by many other sweet dishes. Hannah Glasse suggests pairing stewed pears with it.

It wasn't until the nineteenth century that it became an exclusively sweet and creamy dish as it is most commonly known today.

2½ cups heavy cream
1½ cups whole milk
2 vanilla beans
1½ tablespoons unflavored gelatin
5 tablespoons dark rum
½ cup granulated sugar
3 tablespoons honey

1. In a medium-sized saucepan, stir together the heavy cream, milk, and vanilla beans. Heat until the cream and milk just start to bubble around the sides of the pan, remove from the heat, and let steep 20 minutes.

2. Prepare an ice bath (see Chef's Note, page 85) in a large stainless steel bowl. Bring a small saucepan of water to a simmer. In a metal bowl wider than the small saucepan, sprinkle the unflavored gelatin into the rum, and whisk to combine. Let the gelatin soften for 10 minutes.

3. Whisk the sugar and honey into the cream, and cook the mixture over low heat until the sugar has dissolved. Do not boil.

4. Set the bowl of softened gelatin over the pan of simmering water, stirring constantly until it liquefies. Whisk it into the cream until completely dissolved.

5. Pour the mixture into a heatproof bowl, and set the bowl in the ice bath. Whisk the mixture slowly until cool, allowing it to thicken slightly as it cools. Pour it into a 1-quart Bavarian mold or other gelatin mold. Chill in the refrigerator overnight, so that it can thicken and become firm, before serving.

INDIAN PUDDING

MAKES 10–12 SERVINGS

Although based on traditional English puddings, Indian pudding was uniquely American: It was prepared with cornmeal and often molasses. American cookery books often included recipes for this dish. Hannah Glasse's American edition of *The Art of Cookery Made Plain and Easy*, for example, added two "Indian Pudding" recipes to the section she titled "Several New Receipts Adapted To American Mode of Cooking." Similarly, Amelia Simmons published three versions of "A Tasty Indian Pudding." Inexpensive, sweet, and filling, Indian pudding quickly became a favorite with many Americans, including George Washington and Thomas Jefferson.

Under the heading "Puddings," Thomas Jefferson's collection of recipes included three paragraphs of basic cooking instructions and suggestions for preparing numerous varieties of this sweet dish. As was typical in the period, cake, pastry, biscuits, and so forth were mentioned as suitable bases for successful pudding. Added to this list, however, was the suggestion "For a change with any of the above—you may intermix with fresh or dried fruits, or preserves, even plums, grated cocoanuts, and so on—etc . . ."

The instructions went on to give basic amounts of ingredients and a method of serving the pudding, which was certainly related to the stylish crème caramel:

> When the mould is full of any of the above put into a bowl ¼ teaspoon of either ginger, cinnamon, or mixed spices, or lemon or orange peel. Beat 4 eggs. Add 4 tablespoonfuls of sugar, a pinch of salt and 3 cups of milk. Fill the pudding dish nearly to the rim. It can be either baked, boiled, or set in a saucepan ⅔ full of water, with the lid over, and let simmer for an hour, until set. Run a knife around the edge of the dish and turn out the pudding. Pour over melted butter mixed with some sugar and the juice of a lemon, or serve with brandy sauce.

5 cups whole milk
⅔ cup cornmeal
½ teaspoon salt
1 cup maple syrup
1 tablespoon molasses

4 tablespoons (½ stick) unsalted butter
¾ teaspoon ground ginger
¾ teaspoon ground cinnamon
¼ teaspoon ground mace
1 cup finely chopped dates

1. Preheat the oven to 300°F.

2. Butter a 9 × 13-inch glass baking dish.

3. In a large, heavy-bottomed pot, heat the milk over medium heat.

4. While whisking, slowly sprinkle in the cornmeal.

5. With a wooden spoon or spatula, continue to cook and stir for approximately 10 minutes, until the mixture has thickened.

6. Reduce the heat, add the remaining ingredients, and stir for another 2 minutes.

7. Pour into the prepared baking dish and bake for 2½ hours. Serve warm.

COFFEE CRÈME BRÛLÉE

MAKES 4 SERVINGS

Thomas Jefferson famously fell in love with French cuisine while living in Paris. What is called the City of Light was to Thomas Jefferson the city of culinary delight. Jefferson wasn't alone, though, in diving into luxury and refinement while in France. Voltaire wrote that "in no other city in the world does a larger number of citizens enjoy so much abundance of all good things."

One of the classic "good things" of the French culinary arts is crème brûlée. Here it is combined with coffee, a powerful and taboo beverage during the 1770s, as it came into fashion instead of tea in America and was later blamed for revolutionary uprisings in Europe.

1½ cups heavy cream

3 tablespoons coffee grounds

3½ tablespoons granulated sugar, divided, plus more (about 4 tablespoons) for finishing

4 egg yolks

1. Preheat the oven to 300°F.

2. In a small saucepot over medium heat, simmer the cream with the coffee grounds and 1½ tablespoons of the sugar. Turn off the heat and steep for 15 minutes, or longer for a more intense flavor.

3. In a medium-sized bowl, whisk together the egg yolks and 2 tablespoons of the sugar.

4. Reheat the coffee cream to a simmer, then strain it through a cheesecloth-lined fine mesh strainer to remove the coffee grounds, being sure to squeeze all of the cream out of the cheesecloth.

5. Whisk the warm coffee cream into the egg yolks to combine.

6. Portion into four 4-ounce ramekins set in a baking pan. Place the pan in the oven, pour boiling water into the pan to a depth of 1 inch, and bake in the water bath for approximately 30 minutes or until the custard just barely wobbles in the center.

7. Cool to room temperature and refrigerate until ready to serve.

8. To finish, sprinkle about 1 tablespoon of granulated sugar on top of each custard. With a torch, caramelize the sugar until it is brown but not black and forms a glasslike crust on the custard.

VANILLA BEAN CRÈME BRÛLÉE

MAKES 4 SERVINGS

It was most fashionable to enjoy French desserts in the eighteenth century, particularly among the leaders of America, who were set upon impressing guests with the new nation's sophistication. Great houses in the Americas and Britain prided themselves on having a Frenchman at the helm of the kitchen. Hiring a French chef brought prestige to homes, as he was able to educate the rest of the staff in classical French techniques. French chefs, therefore, commanded a much higher salary than other servants in the home. At the beginning of the eighteenth century in England, the Duke of Bedford paid his French chef sixty pounds a year, while his English chef made only half that. In America, though, kitchens often relied on slave labor. Thomas Jefferson brought his slave cook, James Hemings, to France with him and paid for Hemings to attend culinary school. Upon his return to Virginia, Jefferson boasted about his French-trained chef, who was more than capable of making the pastries and desserts of the day. Crème brûlée was one of the many delicacies that required a special method that Hemings would have learned while living in Paris.

1½ cups heavy cream
3½ tablespoons granulated sugar, divided, plus 4 tablespoons for finishing
1 inch of a vanilla bean, split and scraped
4 egg yolks

1. Preheat the oven to 300°F.

2. In a small saucepan, simmer the cream with 1½ tablespoons of the sugar and the vanilla bean over medium heat.

3. In a medium-sized bowl, whisk together the egg yolks and 2 tablespoons of the sugar.

4. Through a fine mesh strainer, strain the warm cream over the egg yolks and whisk to combine.

5. Portion into four 4-ounce ramekins set in a baking pan. Place the pan in the oven, pour boiling water into the pan to a depth of 1 inch, and bake in the water bath for approximately 30 minutes or until the custard just barely wobbles in the center.

6. Cool to room temperature and refrigerate until ready to serve.

7. To finish, sprinkle 1 tablespoon granulated sugar on top of each custard. Using a torch, caramelize the sugar until it is brown but not black and forms a glasslike crust.

THOMAS JEFFERSON'S FLOATING ISLAND OR SNOW EGGS

MAKES 4 SERVINGS

James Hemings's recipe for "Snow Eggs" written out by Jefferson's granddaughter, Virginia:

> *Take 10 eggs, separate the yolks from the whites and beat the whites as you do for the savoy cake, till you can turn the vessel bottom upward without their leaving it; when they are well beaten put in 2 spoonfuls of powdered sugar and a little orange flower water or rose water if you prefer it. Put a pint of milk in a saucepan with 6 ounces sugar and orange flower or rose water; when your milk boils, take the whites, spoonful by spoonful and do them in the boiling milk; when sufficiently poached, take them out and lay them on a sieve. Take out a part of the milk, according to the thickness you wish to give the custard. Beat up the yolks and stir them in the remainder; as soon as it thickens take the mixture from the fire; strain it through a sieve; dish up your whites and pour the custard over them. A little wine stirred in is a great improvement.*

—JAMES, COOK AT MONTICELLO

While Jefferson gets most of the credit for this dish becoming popular because he so avidly wrote about it, *oeufs à la neige* was a classic favorite among eighteenth-century hosts. Called "Snow and Cream" by some cookbook authors, it was well known for the drastic white color one could achieve by beating the egg whites into a meringue. Author Elizabeth Raffald called it "a pretty supper dish."

In this recipe, we chose to use pear brandy because it accents the orange flower water nicely. Feel free to use your flavor profile of choice: rose water and Madeira, vanilla extract and Grand Marnier, and so on.

1 cup whole milk

1 cup heavy cream

1 tablespoon orange flower water

¾ cup granulated sugar, divided

5 large eggs, separated

2 tablespoons pear brandy

1. In a heavy-bottomed 2-quart saucepan, combine the milk, cream, orange flower water, and ½ cup of the sugar. Set on the stove to be heated later.

2. In the clean, dry bowl of an electric mixer, whip the egg whites on medium speed until foamy. Sprinkle in the remaining ¼ cup of sugar, 1 tablespoon at a time, and whip on high speed until stiff, glossy peaks form.

3. Bring the cream mixture to a simmer, stirring often to avoid scorching.

4. Gently drop large tablespoons of egg white into the hot cream, poach for 2 minutes, and then gently flip the whites over, using a slotted spoon or skimmer. Continue to cook another 2 minutes or until set. The whites will double in volume while cooking, but will shrink down once removed from the hot liquid.

5. Lift the poached whites out of the pot and gently place on a baking sheet to cool. Continue the poaching process until all the egg whites are used.

6. In a medium-sized bowl, whisk the egg yolks until smooth, slowly whisk in 1 cup of the poaching cream, and then return all of the cream and yolks to the pot.

7. Cook over medium-low heat, stirring constantly, until the mixture is thick enough to coat the back of a spoon.

8. Pour the yolk mixture through a fine mesh strainer into a chilled bowl, add the pear brandy, and stir until cool.

9. Place the poached meringues in a serving bowl and pour the custard over them. Serve at room temperature or chilled.

PLUM PUDDING

MAKES 12 SERVINGS

Plum pudding, or Christmas pudding, as it was eventually known, appeared in many variations. Some recipes called for plums, while others called for raisins, currants, and candied lemon and orange peels. In that era, a "plumb" recipe meant it was very rich and expensive. This recipe is akin to the boiled puddings still popular in England. Originally, plumb pudding recipes varied greatly—some required bread crumbs, others, pieces of bread. Boiled puddings could be very simple with few ingredients, and were probably served at a weeknight dinner. Others, such as this one, called for a cupboard full of expensive ingredients, were heavily spiced, and were flavored with liqueur.

What is common to most recipes is the care and time that was required to produce such a rich dessert. These puddings not only demanded a lot of preparation but they also baked or boiled for hours at a time. In addition, until the nineteenth century, suet rather than butter was the fat of choice. Readily available and inexpensive, it not only added flavor but also ensured that the pudding would remain moist through hours of cooking.

Whether baked or boiled, most plum puddings were cooked in decorative molds. Many looked like tall pillars of cake dotted with candied fruit and laced with intricate designs. Like other desserts of the period, when placed among a multitude of offerings, they were meant to add to the beauty and luxuriousness of the sweet table.

1 cup dark raisins

½ cup golden raisins

½ cup currants

1 cup chopped dried pineapple

½ cup dried cherries

½ cup freshly grated unsweetened coconut, toasted

¼ cup almonds, toasted

½ cup chopped candied citrus fruits

¼ cup finely chopped Candied Ginger (see page 191)

Zest of 1 lemon

Zest of 1 lime

1½ cups golden rum, divided

2 cups suet, chopped into ¼-inch pieces, or, if unavailable, lard

2 cups all-purpose flour

4 cups finely crumbled day-old Sally Lunn bread, or any egg bread

1½ teaspoons salt

1 teaspoon ground nutmeg

1 tablespoon ground allspice

1 tablespoon ground cinnamon

Pinch of ground cloves

6 large eggs

1 cup light brown sugar

5 ounces dark beer

1. In a large bowl, toss together the dark and golden raisins, currants, dried fruits, coconut, almonds, candied citrus and ginger, and citrus zests. Add 1 cup of the rum and 2 cups of water; stir to mix. Soak overnight.

2. In a large bowl, cut the suet into the flour, with your fingertips, running the mixture through your fingertips until a coarse meal is formed. In a large bowl, combine the flour-suet mixture with the finely crumbled Sally Lunn bread, salt, nutmeg, allspice, cinnamon, and cloves. Stir to mix well. Add the presoaked fruit mixture, including any liquid in the bowl, and toss until thoroughly combined.

3. In a medium-sized bowl, whisk together the eggs, brown sugar, the remaining ½ cup of rum, and the beer. Add the liquid ingredients to the dry, and mix until a smooth dough is formed. If the mixture seems too dry, add more beer until the dough is smooth.

4. Grease a 2-quart casserole dish or decorative mold with plenty of butter, and lightly dust it with flour.

5. Place the dough in the prepared casserole dish or mold, packing it well. Cover it with foil. Place the mold in a large pot filled with enough water to come halfway up the sides of the dish. Cover the pot with a lid, and bring the water to a simmer on the stove. Keep the water at a simmer, and steam the pudding for 4 hours, checking the water level regularly and refilling as necessary. The pudding is done when it is firm and a toothpick inserted near the center comes out clean.

6. Allow the pudding to cool in the mold at room temperature for about 1 hour. Unmold and serve.

ORANGE FOOL

MAKES 6–8 SERVINGS

The term "fool" is an old English word for a dessert containing sweetened fruit and custard instead of cream. In its earliest forms, a fool included a layer of old cake at the bottom, covered with custard or cream and fruit. By the mid-eighteenth century, that dessert was referred to as a trifle and was much like today's trifles. The fool was a sweetened custard or cream layered with sweetened fruit, such as fresh berries plucked from the vine, gooseberries when in season, or, for the adventurous and wealthy, citrus.

This recipe is inspired by one made popular in Britain in the eighteenth century. It is similar to one served at Boodle's Club, established in 1762, on St. James's Street in London.

1 Vanilla Sponge Cake (see page 206), top evened off and sliced into 3 layers

¼ cup confectioners' sugar

Zest and juice of 2 oranges

Zest of 1 lemon

2 cups heavy cream

Orange segments, for garnish

1. Cut one layer of cake to fit into the bottom of a 1½-quart deep glass bowl or trifle dish.

2. Cut the other cake layers into 1-inch strips and line the sides of the bowl with them, trimming any excess off the top.

3. In a small bowl, mix together the sugar, juice, and zests until the sugar dissolves.

4. In the bowl of an electric mixer with the whisk attachment, whip the heavy cream on medium speed until it just begins to thicken.

5. With the mixer running, stream in the sweetened juices and zest, and whip until all the juice is absorbed and the cream has thickened again.

6. Spoon the flavored cream into the cake-lined bowl, cover, and refrigerate for at least 2 hours before serving.

7. Garnish with orange segments.

APRICOT FOOL

MAKES 6 SERVINGS

The Revolutionary era or, in Britain, the Georgian era saw the rise of countless types of custards and puddings. Hostesses celebrated them for their versatility. Chefs colored them different hues, put them in glasses or bowls, and made elaborate displays with custards and cream. For each variation there was a new name. Be sure to tell guests that a "fool" is on the menu to pique curiosity. This apricot fool is reminiscent of a Popsicle from childhood with flavors of creamy fruit, but it's as elegant as a well-constructed sugar sculpture. Layers of softened apricots are topped with pastry cream and whipped cream, making for a stunning presentation.

9 apricots, pitted and sliced thin
⅓ cup apricot jam
¼ cup packed brown sugar
2 teaspoons grated lemon zest
1 cinnamon stick
1 cup heavy cream
2 tablespoons dry white wine
1 recipe Pastry Cream (see page 202), replacing vanilla extract with orange flower water

1. In a medium-sized saucepan, cook the apricots, jam, brown sugar, zest, and cinnamon over medium heat for approximately 25 minutes, or until the apricots are tender. Transfer the mixture to a bowl and allow to cool to room temperature. Discard the cinnamon stick.

2. In the bowl of an electric mixer with the whip attachment, whisk the heavy cream until soft peaks begin to form. Drizzle in the wine and continue whipping until medium peaks form.

3. Layer the cooked apricot mixture with the whipped cream and pastry cream two or three times, ending with whipped cream on top, in 5-ounce glasses. Refrigerate for at least 1 hour before serving.

PLUM FOOL

MAKES 6 SERVINGS

Plums come in hundreds of shapes, sizes, and colors, although there are only a few varieties readily available in American markets. Stanley and Rosa plums, as mentioned in the recipe, are two of the most commonly sold today. Centuries ago, well before European settlers arrived on this country's shores, Native Americans harvested plums that grew wild on shrubs. Much smaller and tarter than the European kind that colonists brought over, they were better suited for preserves or desserts that had the addition of molasses or sugar to sweeten them, as here. This modern version has much less sugar than those early versions that used native fruits to compensate for the sweeter fruit now available. It is called a fool, as many custard desserts were when layered with fruit and cream.

9 Stanley or Rosa plums, pitted and sliced thin

½ cup apricot jam

⅓ cup packed brown sugar

2 teaspoons grated orange zest

1 cinnamon stick

1½ cups heavy cream

½ teaspoon vanilla extract

1. In a medium-sized saucepot, cook the plums, jam, brown sugar, zest, and cinnamon over medium heat for approximately 25 minutes, or until the plums are tender. Transfer the mixture to a bowl and allow to cool to room temperature. Discard the cinnamon stick.

2. In the bowl of an electric mixer with the whip attachment, whisk the cream until soft peaks begin to form. Drizzle in the vanilla extract and continue whipping until medium peaks form.

3. Layer the cooked plum mixture with the whipped cream two or three times, ending with whipped cream, in 5-ounce glasses. Refrigerate for at least 1 hour before serving.

RICE PUDDING

MAKES 10–12 SERVINGS

The Carolinas were known as much for their rice in the early eighteenth century as they are today for their beaches. Vast plantations were established by colonists, with acre upon acre of rice fields, small ports for shipping, and large, elaborate plantation homes, some that still sit on the water representing their bygone era. By 1726 South Carolina was exporting 4,500 metric tons of rice each year. But the rice did not do well as an export, because it was often broken during the cleaning process. European cooks wanted a cleaner, whiter version, like that found in Italy. During a trip to Lombardy, Thomas Jefferson discovered this much more desirable strain of rice and asked to buy samples. The law forbade export, with a penalty of death for bringing seeds out of the region. "I could only bring off as much as my coat and surtout pockets would hold," he later wrote. Jefferson bribed workmen to smuggle rice seeds out on mules, and later introduced the strain to Virginia in 1787.

4 cups water

1½ cups long-grain white rice

2½ cups whole milk

¾ cup granulated sugar

3 eggs

1½ tablespoons unsalted butter, softened

2 teaspoons vanilla extract

1½ teaspoons ground cinnamon, plus more for garnish

1. Preheat the oven to 425°F.

2. In a 2-quart saucepan, bring the water to a boil and add the rice. Simmer, covered, for about 15 to 20 minutes. Let stand, covered, for 5 minutes and drain, if necessary.

3. In a separate saucepan, bring the milk to a boil. Stir in the drained rice and cook for 10 minutes more, until the grains are soft.

4. In a large bowl, whisk together the sugar, eggs, butter, vanilla, and cinnamon.

5. Gradually stir the hot rice mixture into the egg mixture.

6. Transfer to a 2-quart ovenproof glass or ceramic dish. Place the dish in a larger, high-sided roasting pan, and carefully pour boiling water into the roasting pan around the dish to a depth of 1½ inches. Bake, covered, for about 20 to 30 minutes, until a knife inserted near center comes out clean.

7. Sprinkle additional cinnamon on top as garnish.

SPICED RED CURRANT BREAD PUDDING

MAKES 12 SERVINGS

In the eighteenth century, sweet puddings of many varieties commonly called for the use of pieces of bread, biscuits, or cake as an enriching base for other ingredients, such as dried or fresh fruit or preserves. Bread pudding simply focused on bread (in crumbs or pieces) and custard as primary ingredients, with the typical addition of raisins and spices.

Bread was a staple, baked at home as well as in the many bakeries operating in eighteenth-century America, and period cookbooks suggest that bread pudding was frequently enjoyed. Many bread puddings were boiled, which would be a bit easier than waiting for an oven to cool to the correct temperature. Other recipes had the puddings baked in a crust. The major flavors ranged from the ever-popular rose water to grated lemon zest, and even vinegar combined with butter. Cooks would use the most popular and omnipresent spices of the day—ginger, mace, nutmeg, and cinnamon.

Hannah Glasse's *Art of Cookery Made Plain and Easy* had three recipes for the dish, as did Thomas Jefferson's collection of recipes, which also included two sweet butter sauces to accompany them. This recipe will be familiar to most modern diners, as it is a firm, baked custardlike pudding that uses day-old bread soaked in cream. Feel free to experiment, much like our predecessors would have, based on what's in your cupboard. Try sprinkling in any dried fruit. Bread pudding is always a best seller on the dessert tray at the historic City Tavern. Guests love the seasonal variety, including apricot and white chocolate chunk, blueberry and lemon zest, or coffee and chocolate, depending on the time of year.

½ cup dark rum

1 cup red currants

8 eggs

1 cup brown sugar

1 cup granulated sugar

1 teaspoon salt

2 teaspoons ground cinnamon

2 teaspoons ground ginger

2 teaspoons ground cloves

4 cups half-and-half

18 ounces (10–12 cups) bread, crusts off and cut into 1-inch cubes

1. Preheat the oven to 350°F. Grease a 10-inch springform pan and line it with parchment.

2. Combine the rum and currants in a small bowl and refrigerate for at least 1 hour, or overnight.

3. Whisk together the eggs, sugars, salt, and spices in a large bowl. Slowly whisk in the half-and-half until combined.

4. Place the bread in a large bowl, pour the custard mixture over it, and toss with your hands. Let stand for approximately 10 minutes, or until 80 percent of the liquid has been absorbed.

5. Add the currant and rum mixture to the bread mixture and stir to distribute the currants.

6. Pour into the prepared pan, and cover it with foil. Place the pan in a larger baking or roasting pan, set it in the oven, and pour boiling water into the larger pan to come halfway up the sides of the springform. Bake, in its water bath, for 30 to 40 minutes. Remove the foil and continue to bake for an additional 10 to 15 minutes, or until the custard is set and the top is golden brown.

7. Cool in the springform pan for 5 to 10 minutes. Serve warm.

CHARLOTTE RUSSE

MAKES 10 SERVINGS

This cake is formed of chilled Bavarian cream in a fortress of edible ladyfingers. Still popular in many bakeries for its beautiful presentation, charlotte russe is believed to have been invented by the French chef Marie-Antoine Carême in the late 1700s. Carême penned many intricate recipes for custards and gelatins. While he wrote and spoke in French, he worked in palace kitchens all over Europe.

Carême named this dessert for one of his employers, the Russian czar Alexander I, *russe* meaning "Russian" in French. Many historians believe that the eponymous Charlotte was the czar's sister-in-law, who was wed to Britain's George III. Loyalist Tories in the American colonies most likely continued to bake this confection and affectionately call it Charlotte, but one can imagine patriots renaming it. Just as Freedom Fries popped up in America during the beginning of the Iraq War as a protest to the French government, perhaps the Bluecoats dined on Martha Américaine.

2 (¼-ounce) packets unflavored gelatin

3 tablespoons dark rum

2 cups whole milk

1 tablespoon vanilla extract

8 large egg yolks

½ cup granulated sugar

2½ cups heavy whipping cream

1 recipe Ladyfingers (see page 112), or store-bought ladyfingers

1 cup blueberry preserves (see page 209)

2 pints fresh blueberries

1. Prepare an ice bath (see Chef's Note, page 85) in a large stainless steel bowl. Bring a small pan of water to a simmer.

2. In a somewhat wider metal bowl, sprinkle the unflavored gelatin over the rum and stir to combine. Let the gelatin soften for 10 minutes.

3. In a medium-sized saucepan, combine the milk and vanilla extract; bring to a boil.

4. Meanwhile, in a medium-sized bowl, whisk together the yolks and sugar. Add ¼ cup of the hot milk mixture at a time to the yolks while whisking vigorously. This "tempering" prevents the eggs from scambling in the hot milk. Once the mixtures are completely combined, return the sauce to the pan and cook, stirring constantly, over low heat until the mixture reaches a temperature of 185°F on a candy thermometer and is thick. Strain this custard back into the medium-sized bowl.

5. Dissolve the softened gelatin by setting the bowl over the pan of simmering water, stirring constantly until it liquefies. Whisk the gelatin into the custard. Set the bowl of custard in the ice bath and whisk until the mixture is cool.

6. In the bowl of an electric mixer with the whisk attachment, whip the heavy cream to medium peaks. Add ½ cup of the cool custard to the whipped cream and fold to combine. Fold the remaining custard into the lightened whipped cream.

7. Assemble the charlotte: Spray a 10-inch springform pan and line it with plastic wrap. Put the 9-inch ladyfinger circle in the bottom of the pan. Arrange the ladyfingers around the inside perimeter of the pan, making them stand up like a fence; the 9-inch round should help secure them in place.

8. Fill the ladyfinger-lined pan three-fourths full with the cool Bavarian cream. Freeze for 1 hour.

9. Once the charlotte is frozen, carefully unmold it. Spread the blueberry preserves evenly atop the Bavarian cream. Top the charlotte with the fresh berries.

LADYFINGERS

4 egg yolks

½ cup plus 1 tablespoon granulated sugar, divided

¼ teaspoon lemon juice

5 egg whites

¼ cup plus 1 tablespoon cornstarch

½ cup bread flour

1. Preheat the oven to 350°F. Grease a 9-inch round cake pan and line it with parchment.

2. In the bowl of an electric mixer with the whisk attachment, whip the egg yolks, ¼ cup of the sugar, and the lemon juice with increasing speed until thick and light in color. Transfer to a medium-sized bowl and set aside.

3. Clean and dry the mixer bowl and whisk, add the egg whites, and whip on medium speed until foamy. Gradually add in the remaining 5 tablespoons of sugar, 1 tablespoon at a time, and increase to high speed, whipping the whites to medium-stiff peaks.

4. Gently fold the whipped whites into the lightened yolks in thirds, by hand, until 70 percent incorporated.

5. Combine the cornstarch and flour, sift them over the egg mixture, and gently fold together until combined.

6. Spoon 2 cups of the batter into the prepared cake pan and bake for 7 to 10 minutes, or until a toothpick inserted comes out clean.

7. Line two baking sheets with parchment. Spoon the remaining batter into a piping bag fitted with a ⅜-inch or ⁷⁄₁₆-inch round piping tip, and pipe at least thirty 3-inch-long "fingers" onto the baking sheets. Keep the lines as straight as possible and approximately 1 inch apart. Bake for 7 to 10 minutes or until the fingers are lightly browned and firm to the touch.

RASPBERRY CHARLOTTE ROYALE

MAKES 10 SERVINGS

This dessert has a very similar filling to chef Carême's Charlotte Russe and is a variation on the many desserts made of cake and cream molded together into a pretty form and served chilled. This was very stylish in the day and added another dimension to a sweet table. Traditionally, colonial cooks may have used stale bread dipped in butter to make this cake for fancier occasions that called for a bit more expense and extravagance.

Raspberry Charlotte Royale is a colorful dessert inspired not only by the availability of raspberries in eighteenth-century America but also by the many sponge cake recipes found in cookery books. This cake was a favorite of home cooks and confectioners alike, because it was, and remains, a versatile item whose subtle flavor is married with a variety of fruits and creams.

ROULADE

¾ cup all-purpose flour
¾ teaspoon baking powder
½ teaspoon salt
4 large egg yolks
½ cup plus 6 tablespoons granulated sugar, divided
3 tablespoons corn syrup
4 large egg whites
½ cup framboise or other raspberry-flavored liqueur
1½ cups raspberry preserves (see page 209)

BAVARIAN CREAM

2 (¼-ounce) packets unflavored gelatin
3 tablespoons triple sec, Cointreau, or other orange liqueur
1 tablespoon vanilla extract
1 tablespoon framboise
½ cup granulated sugar, divided
1 cup whole milk
3 large egg yolks
1¼ cups raspberry purée, or frozen raspberries thawed and puréed
2½ cups heavy whipping cream
2 pints fresh raspberries, divided

GLAZE

3 cups Apricot Preserves (see page 210)
1 cup water
Fresh mint sprigs, for garnish

1. Preheat the oven to 400°F. Grease 2 jelly-roll pans with butter, and line them with parchment paper. Grease the parchment as well.

2. Prepare the roulades: Into a large mixing bowl, sift together the flour, baking powder, and salt three times and set it aside.

3. In the bowl of an electric mixer fitted with the whip attachment, whip the egg yolks, ½ cup sugar, and corn syrup on high speed until the mixture is a light color and ribbons form. Transfer the mixture to a medium-sized bowl.

4. Clean and dry the electric mixer bowl and whip attachment immaculately. With the electric mixer on medium speed, whip the whites until foamy.

5. Reduce the mixing speed to low and add the remaining 6 tablespoons of sugar, 2 tablespoons at a time, waiting until each addition incorporates before adding more. Once all the sugar has been added, increase the mixing speed to high, and whip to medium peaks.

6. Transfer 3 tablespoons of the egg white mixture to the yolk mixture, and lightly stir to combine. Using a plastic spatula, fold the remaining whites into the lightened yolk mixture. Next, fold the reserved flour mixture in gently, so as not to deflate the batter.

7. Divide the roulade batter between the two pans and spread it evenly. Bake for 12 minutes, or until the cake is golden and pulls away from sides of the pans. Set on cooling racks to cool.

8. Invert each cake onto the reverse side of a baking pan and remove the parchment. With a pastry brush, soak each cake with framboise liqueur. Using an angled spatula, spread an even amount of preserves on each cake.

9. Starting with a short end, tightly roll each cake. Chill the roulades for 1 hour. Slice each roulade into ½-inch individual jelly rolls.

10. Line a bowl 8 inches wide by 6 inches deep completely with plastic wrap. Line the whole bowl with jelly rolls, starting with the base and working your way up the sides. Pack jelly rolls tightly, leaving no gaps between them.

11. Begin the Bavarian cream: Prepare an ice bath (see Chef's Note, page 85) in a large stainless steel bowl. Bring a small saucepan of water to a simmer. In a slightly wider metal bowl, sprinkle the gelatin over the liqueur and whisk to combine. Let the gelatin soften for 10 minutes.

12. In a medium-sized saucepan, bring the vanilla, framboise, ¼ cup of the sugar, and the milk to a boil.

13. Meanwhile, in a medium-sized bowl, whisk together the yolks and the remaining ¼ cup of sugar. Add ¼ cup at a time of the hot liquid to the yolks, whisking all the while. (This "tempering" prevents the eggs from scambling in the hot milk.) Return the sauce to the pan and cook, stirring constantly, over low heat until the mixture reaches a temperature of 185°F on a candy thermometer and is thick. Strain this custard back into the medium bowl.

14. Dissolve the softened gelatin by setting the bowl over the pan of simmering water, stirring constantly until it liquefies. Whisk the gelatin into the custard.

15. Whisk the raspberry purée into the custard.

16. Set the bowl of custard in the ice bath and whisk until the mixture is cool.

17. In the bowl of an electric mixer with the whisk attachment, whip the heavy cream to medium peaks. Add ½ cup of the cool raspberry custard to the whipped cream and stir gently to combine. Fold the remaining custard into the whipped cream mixture.

18. Fill the jelly-roll-lined bowl with the raspberry Bavarian cream. Stud it with 1 pint of the raspberries by randomly dropping them into the Bavarian cream and letting them sink. Freeze for 1 hour.

19. Prepare the glaze: In a small saucepan, combine the apricot preserves and water; bring to a boil. Remove from the heat and let cool for 10 minutes.

20. Unmold the charlotte onto a serving dish and brush it with the glaze. Garnish with the remaining 1 pint of fresh raspberries and a few sprigs of mint.

Hannah Glasse's Chestnut Pudding

MAKES 6–8 SERVINGS

Adapted from Hannah Glasse's chapter on puddings and fools, this dessert is a rustic example of using the bounty of a season. Chestnuts were readily available all over Europe and in America in autumn. In her original "receipt" or recipe, Mrs. Glasse recommends using cream but instructs the cook who could not procure it to use milk and beat in additional egg yolks.

Mrs. Glasse was not alone in giving flexible instructions, a clue that even in the eighteenth century, cookbook authors realized that recipes are guidelines and would not be followed to a T. Ingredients and skill sets varied widely by region. A reliable supply of rich cream—not needed to separate butter for use in other dishes—would require a certain financial status. However, this pudding could be made by someone of lesser means by substituting a different animal fat and adding egg yolks into the milk to make a creamy pudding. Hannah's recipe is as follows:

> Put a dozen and a half of chestnuts into a skillet or saucepan of water, boil them a quarter of an hour, then blanch and peel them, and beat them in a marble mortar, with a little orange-flower or rose-water and sack, till they are a fine thin paste; then beat up twelve eggs with half the whites, and mix them well, grate half a nutmeg, a little salt, mix them with three pints of cream and half a pound of melted butter; sweeten to your palate, and mix all together; put it over the fire, and keep stirring it till it is thick; lay a puff paste all over the dish, pour in the mixture, and bake it: when you cannot get ream, take three pints of milk, beat up the yolks of four eggs and stir into the milk, set it over the fire, stirring it all the time till it is scalding hot, then mix it in the room of the cream.

3 whole eggs

3 egg yolks

¾ cup chestnut puree (or 18 chestnuts, boiled, peeled, and pureed with approximately ¼ cup water)

½ teaspoon rose water

1½ teaspoons Madeira

⅛ teaspoon freshly grated nutmeg

½ teaspoon salt

3 cups heavy cream

4 ounces (1 stick) melted butter

¾ cup granulated sugar

1. Set up an ice bath (see Chef's Note, page 85).

2. In a medium bowl, whisk the eggs and yolks together until incorporated. Add the chestnut puree, rose water, Madeira, nutmeg, and salt, whisking to combine.

3. Heat the cream, butter, and sugar in a large saucepan over medium heat to a simmer.

4. Take the hot cream mixture off the heat and, ½ cup at a time, whisk it into the egg and chestnut mixture until incorporated.

5. Return the mixture to the pot and cook over low heat, stirring constantly, until the mixture is thick.

6. Pour the hot pudding into the interior bowl of the ice bath and cool to room temperature, stirring occasionally.

7. Portion into one large serving dish or into individual glasses, if desired, and refrigerate for at least 1 hour before serving.

HOLIDAY TRIFLE

MAKES 12 SERVINGS

Modern-day trifles are layers of cake, cream, and berries or chocolates and candies. The term has changed over the centuries. In Shakespeare's day, a trifle was simply a thickened cream flavored with rose water or spices. Eventually, though, it evolved into the elaborate dessert that modern cooks know by that name. It was the cooks and hosts in the middle of the eighteenth century who created versions that twenty-first-century cooks still recognize. This trifle can be made at any time of year, but its use of seasonal ingredients calls to mind the holidays. Gingerbread, cranberries, and whipped cream piled high in a large glass bowl, or made into individual servings in pretty glasses, bring festivity to a table or buffet. However, gingerbread was certainly not reserved for the holiday season in the eighteenth century, so make it whenever the whim strikes.

1 (12-ounce) bag fresh cranberries

Zest of 1 orange

½ cup granulated sugar

1 tablespoon lemon juice

1 cinnamon stick

2 cups heavy cream

⅓ cup confectioners' sugar

½ recipe Orange Anise Biscotti (see page 126)

¼ cup orange liqueur

1 recipe Gingerbread (see page 24), cut into 1-inch cubes

1 recipe Pastry Cream (see page 202)

Candied or dried cranberries, for garnish

Fresh mint, for garnish

1. Place the cranberries, orange zest, sugar, lemon juice, and cinnamon stick in a small bowl and refrigerate overnight.

2. The next day, in the bowl of an electric mixer fitted with the whisk attachment, whip the cream and confectioners' sugar together until medium stiff peaks form.

3. Break the bicotti into small pieces, reserving the smallest for garnish. Lay the biscotti pieces on a baking sheet and generously douse them with orange liqueur.

4. Place a layer of gingerbread cubes in the bottom of your trifle bowl and top it with half of the pastry cream.

5. Add a layer of the moistened biscotti and top it with a layer of cranberries, being sure to use a slotted spoon so as to not drown the trifle in cranberry juice. Top the cranberries with a layer of whipped cream.

6. Repeat the process: gingerbread, pastry cream, biscotti, cranberries, whipped cream.

7. Refrigerate for at least 1 hour before serving. Garnish with candied or dried cranberries, fresh mint, and biscotti crumbles.

BLUEBERRY ORANGE TRIFLE

MAKES 12 SERVINGS

Hannah Glasse wrote instructions for making a trifle that uses Naples biscuits broken into pieces, "macaroons broke in halves, and ratafia cakes. Just wet them through with sack, then make a good boiled custard not too thick, and when cold pour it over it, then put a syllabub over that. You may garnish it with ratafia cakes, currant jelly and flowers."

While the mistress of modern cooking uses three types of hardened biscuits or cookies, we recommend combining cake and cookies for an interesting texture. Her syllabub is sweetened whipped cream with the addition of wine or liqueur—which is as delightful today as it was when she wrote it.

2 cups heavy cream

⅓ cup confectioners' sugar

1 Vanilla Sponge Cake (see page 206), top evened off and cut into 2 layers

1 recipe Pastry Cream (see page 202)

2 pints blueberries

½ recipe Mary Randolph's Shrewsbury Cakes (see page 33), broken into small pieces

4 oranges, segmented

¾ cup orange liqueur, divided

1. In the bowl of an electric mixer with the whisk attachment, whip the cream and sugar together to form medium stiff peaks.

2. Cut one cake layer to fit the bottom of your trifle bowl. Brush with half of the orange liqueur.

3. Top the cake layer with half of the pastry cream, then drop a layer of blueberries over the cream.

4. Top the berries with two-thirds of the Shrewsbury cakes; then spread half of the whipped cream over them. Arrange a layer of orange segments on top of the whipped cream.

5. Begin the process again. Place the remaining cake layer down gently, brush with the remaining orange liqueur, and add the remaining pastry cream, blueberries (reserving a few for garnish), Shrewsbury cakes, whipped cream, and orange segments. Refrigerate for at least 1 hour before serving.

6. Garnish with reserved blueberries and any remaining cake crumbles.

CHAPTER 6

Cookies

SMALL, CRISP CAKES, OR COOKIES, HAVE EXISTED FOR CENTURIES AND HAVE BEEN MADE FAMOUS IN MANY CIRCLES. IN GEORGIAN ENGLAND, JANE AUSTEN WRITES ABOUT MINIATURE CAKES IN *EMMA*, WHILE MARCEL PROUST'S CHARACTER IS TRANSPORTED IN TIME WHEN HE SMELLS AND TASTES THE TINY CAKES CALLED MADELEINES DIPPED IN LIME FLOWER TEA.

Most cookbook writers referred to the miniature delicacies as cakes, not cookies. The name "cookie" probably comes from the New York Dutch who popularized *koekjes*. These small cutouts were baked in outdoor ovens or beehive ovens built into the side of a hearth, or even on a griddle set over coals, and eaten for dessert. Most cooks had recipes for what we now know as cookies, but they didn't call them that at the time.

In fact, Amelia Simmons seems to have been one of the few authors to use the term, in her *American Cookery*. She has recipes for "cookies" and "Another Christmas Cookery." She titled the remaining recipes in this category, however, in the style of contemporaries: primarily as biscuits, drops, and cakes. Some of these cookies remain familiar in America, such as gingerbread and macaroons, while others, with their English roots, are less so, including Naples biscuits, ratafia drops, Savoy cakes, and Shrewsbury cakes.

As today, in colonial America cookies were served on special occasions and for daily treats, enjoyed with "drinking chocolate," wine, rum punch, hard cider, coffee, and liberty tea. The founding fathers drank a glass of milk to accompany their cookies, although the favorites of today, such as chocolate chip and oatmeal raisin, had yet to be invented. Instead people with a sweet tooth were treated to butter cookies, spice cookies, and an array of chewy, crispy, or flaky little desserts.

ALMOND APRICOT COOKIES

MAKES 3 DOZEN

Apricots were much appreciated in the eighteenth century, perhaps because of their limited availability. They were cultivated more successfully in the South's temperate climate than in the North. Both George Washington and Thomas Jefferson had apricot trees in their orchards, and they, like many of their contemporaries, must have enjoyed the fruit not only fresh, in season, but preserved year-round as well.

Martha Washington included a unique recipe for candied apricots in her cookery book. She incorporated "green wheat" into the boiling sugar and fruit, which dyed the apricots a vibrant green, a color admired during the period. This recipe keeps apricots their pretty natural color but will be just as delicious as Martha's.

½ pound (2 sticks) butter

⅜ cup sugar

1 large egg

2⅓ cups all-purpose flour

1 teaspoon baking powder

¼ teaspoon salt

½ cup sliced almonds, toasted

¼ cup Apricot Preserves (see page 210)

⅛ cup unsweetened grated coconut, toasted

¼ cup apricot jam

1. In the bowl of an electric mixer fitted with the paddle attachment, beat the butter and sugar on medium speed until light and fluffy, scraping down the sides of the bowl often. Add the egg and beat well.

2. In a separate bowl, combine the flour, baking powder, and salt.

3. Add the almonds, preserves, and coconut to the mixer bowl and beat well. Add the flour mixture and mix until just combined.

4. Wrap the bowl in plastic wrap and chill in the refrigerator for at least 1 hour, or until easy to handle.

5. Preheat the oven to 350°F.

6. Shape the chilled dough into 1½-inch balls. On an ungreased cookie sheet, place the dough balls 1 inch apart.

7. Press your thumb into the center of each dough ball. Place ½ teaspoon of apricot jam in the impression.

8. Bake for 12 to 15 minutes, or until the edges are lightly browned. Transfer the cookies to a wire rack and let cool.

MADELEINES

MAKES 2 DOZEN

These pretty little cakelike delicacies are impressive but not complicated to make. There are many stories swirling among food historians about how they came to be called madeleines. Most people agree that the cookies are certainly from the town of Commercy in the Lorraine region of France. But that's where the story frays. Some historians say that a convent of Catholic nuns in Commercy baked and sold them to support their abbey, which was named for Mary Magdalene, or Marie-Madeleine in French. As the cookies grew in popularity and people traveled with them outside the region, they became known by the name of the abbey. Others believe that a servant named Madeleine baked them for the exiled king of Poland when he was banished to Commercy in the early 1700s. The cookies were then enjoyed by royal families throughout Europe, who named the treats after the original cook. Either way, they are most delicious and sure to please.

¼ cup sugar

Zest of 1 lemon

4 large egg yolks

¼ pound (1 stick) unsalted butter, melted

3 large egg whites

¼ cup all-purpose flour

1. Grease a madeleine tray and coat lightly with flour. Preheat the oven to 375°F.

2. Place the sugar in a small bowl and grate the lemon zest over it.

3. In the bowl of an electric mixer fitted with the whip attachment, whip the egg yolks and the lemon zest–sugar mixture on medium speed until it triples in volume and ribbons form. Slowly mix in the butter.

4. Transfer the whipped yolks to a medium-sized stainless steel bowl.

5. Clean the electric mixer bowl and whip attachment and dry thoroughly. Add the egg whites, and whip to stiff peaks.

6. In a medium-sized bowl, sift the flour three times. Fold the flour into the yolk mixture, about 1 tablespoon at a time.

7. Carefully spoon one-third of the yolk mixture into the whipped egg whites. Fold the egg white mixture into the yolk mixture, being careful not to deflate the batter.

8. Fill the madeleine molds half full.

9. Bake for 5 to 7 minutes, or until golden and puffed double in size. Remove from the oven and turn the molds upside down to remove all the cakes immediately. Do not allow to cool in the molds. Serve at room temperature.

ORANGE ANISE BISCOTTI

MAKES APPROXIMATELY 18

Originally called *biscottini*, or "little biscuits," these were hard, dry biscuits for sailors made by cutting bread and baking it a second time so it would last on a sea voyage. The breads were sometimes flavored or sweetened, which evolved into modern biscotti. For centuries, anise has been one of the most traditional additions to biscotti, and it was certainly a popular spice in the eighteenth century. Like many other imported spices and foodstuffs, anise seeds were readily available in shops and markets.

⅔ cup granulated sugar

⅓ cup vegetable oil

1 large egg

¼ cup sour cream

½ teaspoon orange extract

2¼ cups sifted all-purpose flour

½ teaspoon baking powder

½ teaspoon baking soda

½ teaspoon salt

½ teaspoon crushed anise seed

½ teaspoon orange zest

1. Preheat the oven to 350°F. Line a cookie sheet with parchment paper.

2. In the bowl of an electric mixer fitted with the paddle attachment, beat the sugar, oil, and egg on medium speed until combined, scraping down the sides of the bowl often. Add the sour cream and orange extract, and beat well.

3. In a separate bowl, sift together the flour, baking powder, baking soda, and salt. Stir in the anise seed and orange zest. With the mixer on low, slowly add the dry ingredients to the wet ingredients.

4. Transfer the dough to a lightly floured surface, and knead the dough with your hands for 1 minute.

5. Shape the dough into a 12-inch roll about 2 inches in diameter, and place the roll in the center of the prepared cookie sheet.

6. Bake for 20 to 25 minutes, or until light golden brown.

7. Remove from the oven. Cool on the cookie sheet for about 25 minutes. Using a serrated knife, cut the log into 1½-inch-thick diagonal slices.

8. Arrange the slices, flat sides down, on the same cookie sheet, and put back into the oven for 5 minutes. Turn each slice over and bake 5 minutes more until the biscotti are just toasted. Do not overbake.

9. Transfer the biscotti to a wire rack and let cool. To store, transfer them to a tightly covered container and keep at room temperature.

Spritz Cookies

MAKES 2 DOZEN

A sweet, buttery flavor and fanciful shape define these cookies of northern European origin. The soft dough is pushed through a special cookie press, hence the name, from *spritzen*, German for "to squirt or spray." These festive cookies in different shapes and sizes are typical of Germany and Scandinavia. As settlers came to the American colonies from those regions, they brought their appetites and customs with them. Many varieties of butter cookies existed in the New World, and these would have made special appearances in eastern European neighborhoods in cosmopolitan cities. They were very popular in the eighteenth century and saw a resurgence in the 1970s, when American bicentennial fever took the nation.

¾ cup granulated sugar

8½ ounces (2 sticks plus 1 tablespoon) unsalted butter, softened

1 teaspoon vanilla extract

1 medium egg

3 tablespoons heavy cream

3 cups cake flour, sifted

½ teaspoon salt

1. Cream the sugar, butter, and vanilla in a mixer on medium speed for 15 minutes.

2. Add the egg, scrape down the sides of the mixing bowl, and beat until incorporated.

3. With the mixer running, stream in the cream and mix until incorporated.

4. Add the flour and salt and mix slowly until just combined.

5. Spoon the dough into a pastry bag fitted with a large star tip or into a cookie press and gently squeeze the dough out into stars, swirls, or 2-inch lines.

6. Chill the piped cookies for 10 to 15 minutes. Preheat the oven to 300°F.

7. Bake for 7 to 10 minutes until firm and just beginning to brown. Remove from oven and let cool on a tray for 5 to 10 minutes. Remove from trays with a spatula and allow to finish cooling on a wire rack. Store in an airtight container.

SPICE COOKIES

MAKES ABOUT 3 DOZEN

Most eighteenth-century cookies, or "cakes" as they were called during that period, were seasoned with spices. Whole or ground caraway and coriander seeds ranked among the most popular. As in these cookies, nutmeg, ginger, and cinnamon were added to a variety of baked goods to add a taste of the exotic and a depth of flavor to simple preparations. This recipe recalls crisp varieties of gingerbread that came from the kitchens of many colonial American homes and bakeshops. Many shops in bustling port cities carried imported foodstuffs that were incorporated into desserts.

On April 14, 1790, for example Cadwalder & David Evans advertised in the *Pennsylvania Gazette* that "At their Store, the south side of Market street, the second door below Fifth street" they had for sale imported "Pepper, allspice, ginger, cinnamon [and] cloves" as well as the ever-popular "Anniseed."

8 ounces (2 sticks) unsalted butter, softened
⅔ cup granulated sugar
½ cup molasses
2 egg yolks
2½ cups all-purpose flour
1½ teaspoons ground cinnamon
1½ teaspoons ground ginger
½ teaspoon ground allspice
⅛ teaspoon ground cloves
½ teaspoon salt
Sanding or granulated sugar, for rolling
   (optional)

1. Preheat the oven to 325°F.

2. In the bowl of an electric mixer with the paddle attachment, cream the butter and sugar until light and fluffy.

3. Scrape down the sides of the bowl, add the molasses, and continue beating until the molasses is incorporated.

4. Add the yolks and mix until incorporated, scraping down the bowl once or twice.

5. Sift together the dry ingredients except sugar for rolling; then add them to the butter mixture all at once. Starting on low speed, pulse the mixer to gently incorporate the flour. Gradually increase the speed, scraping down the bowl between increases, and mix until all of the flour is absorbed.

6. Scoop the dough with an ice cream scoop onto a parchment-lined baking sheet and refrigerate for 5 to 10 minutes or until you can handle the dough. Roll each scoop in sanding (or granulated) sugar, return to the baking sheet, and bake for 12 to 15 minutes, or until golden and mostly firm to the touch.

7. Cool the cookies completely on the baking sheet. Store in an airtight container at room temperature for up to 3 days.

PINE NUT COOKIES

MAKES 2 DOZEN

These cookies are yet another variation of the many butter cookies baked in the eighteenth century with a crunchy, savory addition. Pine nuts are actually the seeds of pine trees, and there are many varieties, although the Italian pignoli are most commonly sold today. Native Americans ate pine nuts raw or roasted, and some tribes ground roasted pine nuts and mixed them with cornmeal to make breads and cakes, particularly in the Southwest.

2 cups pine nuts

½ cup plus 2 tablespoons almond paste

6 tablespoons honey

8 ounces (2 sticks) unsalted butter, cubed, at room temperature

½ cup granulated sugar

4 large eggs

4 large egg yolks

1¼ cups plus 2 tablespoons sifted all-purpose flour

1 cup finely ground toasted almonds

1. Preheat the oven to 325°F. Line two cookie sheets with parchment paper.

2. Place the pine nuts on a baking pan and toast in the oven for 5 minutes, checking frequently, until light golden. Set aside to cool completely.

3. In the bowl of an electric mixer fitted with the paddle attachment, mix the almond paste with the honey on low speed until soft and smooth. Scrape down the sides of the bowl.

4. With the mixer still running on low speed, add the butter by the cube. Scrape down the sides of the bowl when half the butter has been added. Once all the butter has been added, scrape down the sides of the bowl again, add the sugar, and mix on medium speed until smooth.

5. With the mixer still on medium speed, add the eggs and yolks, one at a time. Mix until smooth. Scrape down the sides of the bowl.

6. Shut off the mixer and add the flour, ground almonds, and toasted pine nuts. Pulse the mixture just until it comes together. Scrape down the sides of bowl, making sure the mixture is homogeneous.

7. Drop the batter by the tablespoonful, at 1-inch intervals, onto the prepared cookie sheets.

8. Bake for 7 to 8 minutes, or until the sides just begin to turn light golden. Let cool on the cookie sheets for 10 minutes. Allow to cool completely. Store in airtight containers at room temperature for up to 1 week.

FINANCIERS
MAKES ABOUT 18

Financiers, rich cookies shaped like tiny gold bars, are made with ground almonds, a nut that has been enjoyed in sweet and savory preparations since prehistoric times. English cookery books have had recipes that use ground almonds to make flour and marzipan since the Middle Ages, when marzipan was a very fashionable dessert. In the seventeenth century, European royalty enjoyed pies containing almonds and meats and lots of exotic spices. Later almonds became popular in sweet preparations. It wasn't until the eighteenth century that almond trees were introduced to America. Franciscan priests planted them in coastal California as part of their missions.

⅔ cup almond flour
½ cup all-purpose flour (agitated and spooned into cup, then evened off)
1⅙ cups confectioners' sugar
3½ egg whites
6 tablespoons brown butter, cooled to room temperature

1. Combine the dry ingredients in the bowl of an electric mixer. With the paddle attachment, slowly incorporate the egg whites, scraping down the sides of the bowl often. Mix until just combined.

2. Slowly drizzle in the cooled brown butter and mix until just combined.

3. Refrigerate the dough for at least 1 hour.

4. Preheat the oven to 325°F.

5. Spray miniature muffin tins or miniature silicon baking molds with nonstick spray, and pipe or spoon the batter into each cavity until three-quarters full.

6. Bake until golden and firm in the center, 15 to 20 minutes. Cool in their molds, and store in an airtight container at room temperature.

PISTACHIO CRESCENTS

MAKES 18 CRESCENTS

Buttery crescent-shaped nut cookies exist in numerous cultures and were introduced to America as immigrants arrived throughout the centuries. This version is simply and richly flavored with ground pistachios, vanilla, and butter and delicately dusted with confectioners' sugar. Pistachios have been an addition to menus for centuries—the ancient Greeks ate them. The nut trees are originally from central Asia, but spread to Italy in the first century and to the American colonies as Italians visited the shores of the nation.

½ cup shelled pistachio nuts

1¾ cups all-purpose flour

1 vanilla bean

1 pound confectioners' sugar, divided

½ pound (2 sticks) unsalted butter, cubed, at room temperature

3 large egg yolks

1. Preheat the oven to 350°F.

2. Arrange the pistachios in a single layer on a cookie sheet. Toast in the oven for about 5 minutes. Turn off the oven, remove the pistachios, and let cool for about 10 minutes. Transfer the pistachios to the bowl of a food processor, add 2 tablespoons of the flour, and process until finely ground.

3. Slice the vanilla bean in half lengthwise. Using the back of a knife, scrape the seeds from each half. In a small bowl, combine ¾ cup of the confectioners' sugar and the vanilla seeds.

4. In the bowl of an electric mixer fitted with the paddle attachment, beat the butter and the vanilla-sugar mixture on medium speed until smooth. Scrape down the sides of the bowl.

5. With the mixer on medium speed, add the yolks one at a time, beating after each addition. Scrape down the sides of the bowl.

6. Remove the bowl from the mixer, and with a rubber spatula or wooden spoon, fold in the remaining flour and the ground pistachios.

7. Scrape the dough onto a lightly floured countertop, and knead a few times until smooth. Roll the dough into three logs, 1 inch thick and 12 inches long. Wrap the logs in plastic wrap, and chill in the refrigerator for 2 hours.

8. Lightly dust the countertop with flour, and unwrap the cookie dough. Using a chef's knife or bench scraper, cut each log into 2-inch-long pieces. With your left and right index fingers, roll out each piece slightly and taper the edges somewhat. Bend the edges in, creating a half moon. It is easier to work with cold dough, so if the dough becomes difficult to work with, return it to the refrigerator to chill for a few minutes. Try to avoid using too much dusting flour, because this will dry out the cookies.

9. Line up the cookies, 1 inch apart, on two cookie sheets. Transfer the cookie sheets to the refrigerator to chill for 30 minutes.

10. Preheat the oven to 350°F.

11. Transfer the chilled cookie sheets to the oven and bake for about 8 minutes. While the cookies are in the oven, fill a bowl with the remaining ¼ cup of confectioners' sugar.

12. When the cookies are light golden, remove them from the oven and let them cool slightly. While the cookies are still warm, roll them in the bowl of confectioners' sugar, covering them well.

13. On cooling racks, allow the cookies to cool completely; then dust again with confectioners' sugar.

Mrs. Goodfellow's Jumbles

MAKES APPROXIMATELY 2 DOZEN

Mrs. Goodfellow was a famous baker and operated the first cooking school in America in Philadelphia. Her pupils were the daughters of the city's finest and richest, who had to learn the necessities of operating a kitchen, overseeing a staff of cooks, and managing ingredients. Many of her desserts relied on classic and very popular ingredients that appear regularly in the eighteenth century and in this cookbook—the showstopping standards of the day—such as nutmeg, rose water, and brandy. She would have demonstrated this recipe, as well as many others, to her students, thus giving them a better idea of how to measure the proportions of wine, brandy, and rose water. At the very least, the well-dressed and well-heeled young ladies would have observed her measurements, as the original recipes were not exact, but called for a "cup full" or a "glass."

8 ounces (2 sticks) unsalted butter, softened
1 cup granulated sugar
Zest of ½ lemon
2 eggs
1 teaspoon ground mace
1⅔ cups all-purpose flour
1¼ ounces rose water

1. Preheat the oven to 325°F.

2. In the bowl of an electric mixer with the paddle attachment, cream the butter, sugar, and lemon zest until light and fluffy.

3. Add the eggs one at a time, scraping down between each addition.

4. In a small bowl sift together the mace and flour, then add it to the mixer.

5. Drizzle in the rose water and mix until all the flour is absorbed.

6. Spoon or pipe the dough into miniature muffin tins or small silicon molds and bake for 12 to 15 minutes, until lightly golden and firm to the touch.

7. Allow jumbles to cool in the pan, then turn out and store in an airtight container at room temperature.

FRENCH MACAROONS

MAKES APPROXIMATELY 18

Try filling these cookies with buttercream for a classic taste, or whipped ganache, jam, or your favorite nut butter for a personal twist. French macaroons have been popular as a building base for desserts for centuries. In 1656, French chefs suggested making tortes by soaking macaroons in red wine and garnishing with candied lemon. Later, in the eighteenth century, Hannah Glasse and Mary Randolph called for them to make a trifle layered with cream and fruit. They are also delicious served with coffee or tea or enjoyed on their own.

2½ egg whites
⅓ cup granulated sugar
6 ounces almond paste, at room temperature

1. Preheat the oven to 375°F.

2. In the bowl of an electric mixer with the paddle attachment, beat half of the whites with the sugar until a paste forms.

3. Add the almond paste and mix in until completely smooth. This is a key step: Make sure there are no lumps before continuing.

4. Gradually add the remaining egg whites with the mixer running. Add only enough whites to achieve a dough that can be piped—it should not be runny.

5. On a parchment-lined baking sheet or a silicon mat, pipe 1½-inch rounds evenly spaced. Let stand at room temperature for 5 to 10 minutes.

6. Reduce the oven temperature to 325°F and bake for 10 minutes, or until crisp and firm. If working in batches, raise the oven temperature to 375°F for 5 minutes between each round, reducing it back to 325°F before baking.

7. Allow the macaroons to cool on the baking sheet for 2 to 3 minutes before transferring them to a wire rack to cool completely.

8. When the cookies have cooled completely, sandwich them together with the filling of your choice.

LINZER COOKIES

MAKES 18-24

These pretty treats are miniature linzer tortes. The eponymous dessert hails from Linz, Austria, and made its way to America's shores first in the larger form, about the size of a pie, with lattice crust. Desserts layered with several components, such as linzer tortes, were quite the accomplishment in the eighteenth century because cooks had to make raspberry jam first, then grind freshly roasted nuts and begin the process of making the dough. Linzer cookies are still popular today in bakeries and at home because of their sweet-tart raspberry filling and crunchy, nut-laden crust.

8 ounces (2 sticks) unsalted butter

¾ cup granulated sugar

1 large egg

½ teaspoon vanilla extract

2 cups cake flour, sifted

½ teaspoon ground cinnamon

1¼ cup sliced almonds, toasted and finely ground

1 egg whisked with 1 tablespoon water, to be used as a wash

¾ cup raspberry jam

1. In the bowl of an electric mixer with the paddle attachment, cream the butter and sugar until light and fluffy.

2. Scrape down the sides of the bowl, add the egg, and mix until combined.

3. Add the vanilla, mix, and scrape down the sides of the bowl again.

4. Add the dry ingredients and carefully mix until just combined.

5. Wrap the dough in plastic wrap and refrigerate for at least 1 hour.

6. Preheat the oven to 350°F.

7. On a lightly floured surface, roll half of the dough to ¼-inch thickness. Using a fluted 2½-inch cookie cutter, cut eighteen rounds and space them evenly on a parchment-lined baking sheet.

8. Roll the other half of the dough to ¼-inch thickness and cut eighteen more rounds. Then cut the center out of each round with a 1½-inch or 2-inch cutter. Brush each round on the baking sheet with the egg wash, then gently place on it a round with the center cut out, creating a well for the jam.

9. Pipe or spoon the jam into the center of each cookie, brush again with the egg wash, and refrigerate for 10 minutes before baking.

10. Bake for 12 to 15 minutes or until golden. Cool on the baking sheet to room temperature. Store in an airtight container at room temperature.

CHEF'S NOTE

You can reroll the dough once more before it becomes too tough, or bake off the trimmings as they are and dip them in chocolate for a "chef's treat."

GINGERBREAD COOKIES
MAKES APPROXIMATELY 2 DOZEN

Gingerbread is a well-loved German tradition that was especially important in the city of Nuremberg. Recipes for small, crisp Pfefferkuchen, or "pepper cakes" popped up as early as the 1690s. Original recipes called for distilled cinnamon water; however, this more updated recipe makes do with familiar ingredients, such as a combination of warm spices—allspice, cloves, nutmeg, and ginger. Colonial cooks most often carved shapes from the dough, making commemorative saints for feast days. For people who could not afford gingerbread men, bakers often made "snaps" from the scraps of dough.

2 ounces (½ stick) unsalted butter, softened
¼ cup dark brown sugar
¼ cup granulated sugar
1 tablespoon grated fresh ginger
2⅞ cups all-purpose flour
1⅛ teaspoons baking soda
1½ teaspoons ground ginger
½ teaspoon ground allspice
¼ teaspoon ground cloves
¼ teaspoon freshly grated nutmeg
¼ teaspoon ground cardamom
¼ cup molasses
2 tablespoons honey
2 tablespoons maple syrup
¼ cup apple cider

1. In the bowl of an electric mixer with the paddle attachment, cream the butter and sugars until light and fluffy. Add the fresh ginger and continue creaming, scraping down the sides of the bowl occasionally.

2. In a separate bowl sift together all of the dry ingredients.

3. In another small bowl, dissolve the molasses, honey, and maple syrup into the apple cider.

4. Add the dry ingredients to the butter mixture and carefully begin to mix together on low speed.

5. Drizzle in the cider-syrup with the mixer running, and mix until all the flour and cider are absorbed.

6. Cover the dough with plastic wrap and refrigerate for at least 1 hour or until firm enough to work with.

7. Preheat the oven to 325°F.

8. On a floured surface, roll out the dough approximately ¼ inch thick. Use a knife or cookie cutters to achieve the desired shapes, evenly space them on parchment-lined baking sheets, and bake for 10 to 12 minutes or until golden brown and firm to the touch.

9. Cool the cookies on the baking sheet, and store in an airtight container at room temperature.

CHEF'S NOTE

After rolling out the cookie dough, cut out cookies as close together as possible for maximum efficiency. You can reroll the dough twice, but beyond that it can become tough and nearly inedible.

CHAPTER 7

Quick Breads

BREADS SWEETENED WITH FRUITS AND SPICES WERE SLICED, BUTTERED, AND LIGHTLY SPICED FOR BREAKFAST AND FOR MORE MODEST TEATIME SWEET TABLES. SOMETIMES, COOKS BAKED THE RECIPES IN SMALL TINS.

Muffins originated in the 1770s in northern Britain, and some estates even purchased them for breakfast and supper from local bakers. Biscuits had been in dining rooms and at tea tables for many years by the eighteenth century, so creative cooks found new ingredients, including fruit and nuts, to add to the basic flour-and-butter recipes.

The recipes reflect cake recipes more than bread, because there is no yeast, no rising, no kneading, and much less work than bread. In the eighteenth century these breads were referred to as cakes and biscuits, some of which were prepared with "emptins," which was a fermented leavener based on flour and ale. Quick breads rely on fast-acting leaveners, including baking powder, baking soda, and, in the case of light batters, eggs.

Although chemical leaveners were not widely available until the nineteenth century, eighteenth-century bakers used pearl ash or pot ash (early forms of baking soda) to ensure that their cakes and biscuits would rise quickly.

Referring to breads that bake quickly with no yeast as quick breads is part of the American baker's vocabulary, but it's uncertain when "quick bread" became the one-size-fits-all term it is today. Whatever our founding foodies called them, eighteenth-century cooks made them in abundance as a means of using overripe fruit, just as frugal cooks do today.

Ginger Raisin Scones

MAKES APPROXIMATELY 1 DOZEN

Raisins were a delicacy in the eighteenth century because they were imported from Europe, so they were featured in very special desserts and pastries. Just like rum and sugarcane, raisins were a large part of the triangular trade between the Americas, Africa, and Europe. Spanish missionaries also brought dried figs and raisins to San Diego when settling California, so the sweet, dried treats were available on both of the continent's shores. Although California did not join the United States until 1850, people living in the territories exported their crops to the earlier states.

2 cups all-purpose flour

⅓ cup packed dark brown sugar

1 tablespoon baking powder

¾ teaspoon ground cinnamon

1 teaspoon ground ginger

1 pinch ground cloves

6 tablespoons (¾ stick) unsalted butter, at room temperature

¼ cup whole milk

3 tablespoons dark molasses

1 large egg

1 teaspoon vanilla extract

1 tablespoon grated fresh ginger

⅔ cup raisins (plumped overnight in water, drained before use)

1. Preheat the oven to 375°F.

2. In a large mixing bowl, combine the flour, brown sugar, baking powder, and spices.

3. In a medium-sized mixing bowl, combine the butter, milk, molasses, egg, vanilla, and grated ginger.

4. Add the egg mixture to the dry ingredients and stir until just moistened. With a rubber spatula or wooden spoon, gently fold in the raisins.

5. Turn the dough out onto a lightly floured surface and roll approximately 1 inch thick. Cut scones out using a 3-inch round cookie or biscuit cutter and evenly space them on a parchment-lined baking sheet.

6. Bake 20 to 25 minutes, or until golden brown, and serve warm.

Sweet Potato Biscuits

MAKES ABOUT 2 DOZEN BISCUITS

Sweet potatoes were plentiful in the southern colonies, and the renowned gardener Thomas Jefferson participated enthusiastically in their cultivation, along with many farmers in the warm southern climes. George Washington, in fact, was one of them. This root vegetable makes a number of appearances in Jefferson's collection of recipes and inspired the recipe here. Sweet potatoes contribute a sweet flavor and light texture to these biscuits and are complemented by the addition of one of Jefferson's other favorite foods: pecans.

5 cups all-purpose flour

1 cup packed light brown sugar

2 tablespoons baking powder

1½ teaspoons ground cinnamon

1 teaspoon salt

1 teaspoon ground ginger

½ teaspoon ground allspice

1 cup vegetable shortening

2 cups cooked, mashed, and cooled sweet potato (about 2 large potatoes)

1 cup heavy cream

½ cup coarsely chopped pecans

1. Preheat the oven to 400°F.

2. In a large mixing bowl, place the flour, brown sugar, baking powder, cinnamon, salt, ginger, and allspice; stir to combine.

3. Add the shortening, and cut in with two knives or a pastry cutter until crumbly.

4. Add the sweet potato, and mix well with a wooden spoon. Add the cream and pecans, and stir just until moistened.

5. Turn the dough out onto a lightly floured surface. Roll out the dough to ½ inch thickness. Cut out biscuits with a 2-inch floured biscuit cutter. Place the biscuits 1 inch apart on ungreased baking pans.

6. Set the pans in the oven, reduce the oven temperature to 350°F, and bake 25 to 30 minutes or until golden brown. Serve warm or let cool on a wire rack to room temperature.

CHEF'S NOTE

The biscuit dough freezes beautifully unbaked. Just layer the dough between sheets of waxed paper and store for up to 3 months. Defrost the dough and follow the baking directions. It pays to make a double batch of these biscuits and freeze half for another occasion.

BANANA NUT BREAD

MAKES 1 (8.5 X 4-INCH) LOAF

Bananas were originally shipped to the American colonies from the Caribbean in merchant vessels returning from the islands with rum, fruit, and spices on the triangle trade. It sometimes took days to get into port, so bananas that were picked green could be very ripe when they arrived. Bananas were often baked into bread instead of eaten raw, because the ripe fruit quickly turned brown and soft. Frugal eighteenth-century cooks would never let this delicacy go to waste, so recipes for banana bread were prevalent in the colonies. Recipes that used overripe fruit were a means to prolong the delicious flavor of the island treasure.

⅓ cup vegetable oil

⅔ cup granulated sugar

⅙ cup sour cream

3 overripe bananas

1 egg

1 cup all-purpose flour

½ teaspoon baking soda

½ teaspoon baking powder

½ teaspoon salt

½ teaspoon cinnamon

½ tablespoon vanilla

⅙ cup golden rum

½ cup chopped walnuts

Sanding or granulated sugar, for sprinkling

1. Preheat the oven to 375°F. Grease one 8.5 x 4-inch loaf pan.

2. Mix the oil, sugar, sour cream, bananas, and egg by hand with a wooden spoon or in the bowl of an electric mixer with the paddle attachment.

3. Combine the dry ingredients, then add to the wet mixture and mix until just combined.

4. Add the vanilla, rum, and nuts and mix just until all ingredients are moistened.

5. Pour into the loaf pan, sprinkle with sugar, and bake for 30 to 45 minutes, or until a toothpick inserted in the center comes out clean.

PINEAPPLE RUM BREAD

MAKES 1 (8.5 X 4-INCH) LOAF

Pineapple has been a symbol of hospitality for centuries. Shipped in from the West Indies in the eighteenth century, pineapple was an expensive luxury in colonial seaports, so hostesses offered it as a compliment to their important guests, carefully arranged on sweet tables. For an eighteenth-century woman, table display was a means of declaring her personality and her family's status. Hostesses sought to outdo each other in the creation of memorable, fantasy-like dining room scenes, and the pineapple was the crowning fruit in many displays. When the exotic fruits turned, the woman of the house would have her cooks use them as ingredients in breads or compotes.

1 egg
1 egg yolk
1 cup granulated sugar
½ cup vegetable oil
8 ounces crushed pineapple, drained
1½ cups all-purpose flour
½ teaspoon baking soda
½ teaspoon cinnamon
½ teaspoon salt
½ teaspoon vanilla
¼ cup rum
Sanding sugar or granulated sugar, for sprinkling

1. Preheat the oven to 375°F. Grease one 8.5 × 4-inch loaf pan.

2. Cream together the eggs and sugar by hand with a wooden spoon, or in the bowl of an electric mixer with the paddle attachment.

3. Add the oil and crushed pineapple, then dry ingredients, mixing until almost combined.

4. Add vanilla and rum and mix just until all ingredients are moistened.

5. Pour into the loaf pan, sprinkle with sanding sugar, and bake for 30 to 45 or until a toothpick inserted in the center come out clean.

PUMPKIN RAISIN BREAD

MAKES 1 (8.5 X 4-INCH) LOAF

Pumpkins grew plentifully in North America and were cultivated first by Native Americans and later by the colonists. They are native and in season year-round in the Caribbean, where the outsides of the fruits are green, not orange as in North America. Pumpkin—or "pompion," as early Americans and Europeans often called it—was not only commonly incorporated into puddings and pies but was also candied, as in Harriet Pinckney Horry's recipe "To make Pompion Chips."

¾ cup pumpkin puree

¼ cup vegetable oil

¼ cup water

1 cup granulated sugar

1 egg

1 egg yolk

1⅙ cups all-purpose flour

½ teaspoon baking soda

½ teaspoon salt

⅛ teaspoon nutmeg

1 teaspoon cinnamon

½ teaspoon vanilla

⅓ cup raisins soaked in ½ cup dark rum overnight (rum reserved)

1. Preheat the oven to 375°F. Grease one 8.5 x 4-inch loaf pan.

2. Mix together the pumpkin, oil, water, sugar, and eggs, either by hand with a wooden spoon or in the bowl of an electric mixer with the paddle attachments.

3. Combine the dry ingredients, then add to the pumpkin mixture and mix until just combined.

4. Add the vanilla, raisins, and rum, and mix just until all ingredients are moistened.

5. Pour into the loaf pan and bake for 30 to 45 or until a toothpick inserted in the center come out clean.

CHAPTER 8

Pastries

While America had its roots in British cuisine because of its founding sovereign, the new country quickly reached for the more cosmopolitan style of French cookery. England was regularly at war with France, so the enemy nation's food was in and out of style as politics dictated. Americans, however, were free to enjoy the inspiration of all things French.

The alliance between France and America in 1778 led patriots to celebrate its brother in arms by replicating its fashion and culinary arts. When the Marquette de Lafayette toured America in 1784 at George Washington's invitation, French cuisine was elevated even higher in the eyes of many patriots.

The country was also being inundated with new citizens fleeing the French Revolution or striving to find a new home in a foreign land based on the same ideals of democracy. More French people fled the colony of Haiti during the slave rebellion of the 1790s and relocated to the new United States. They brought with them a great knowledge and love of pastry making.

Skills associated with the preparation of pastry were much admired in the eighteenth century. Bakers were familiar with many types of dough and "paste."

While patriots were carving out a name for America as a sophisticated food culture, the country's elite hosts were keeping up with Marie Antoinette's love of cakes and sweet treats. It would never do for the French court to have more elaborate confections than America's founding fathers.

Despite her apparent dislike of French fashion, Eliza Smith clearly acknowledged the importance of French-inspired recipes in *The Compleat Housewife*, as she discussed in her preface:

What you will find in the following Sheets, are Directions generally for dressing after the best, most natural and wholesome Manner, such Provisions as are the Product of our own Country; and in such a Manner as is most agreeable to English Palates; saving that I have so far temporized, as, since we have, to our Disgrace, so fondly admired the French Tongue, French Modes, and also French Messes, to present you now and then with such Receipts of the French Cookery as I think may not be disagreeable to English Palates.

MILLE-FEUILLE

MAKES 8 SERVINGS

French for "thousand-leaf," this dessert traditionally consists of three layers of puff pastry and two layers of whipped cream or pastry cream. The top piece of pastry is often decoratively finished with a liberal sprinkling of confectioners' sugar or a thin coating of fondant.

Each component of the mille-feuille is prepared separately and used to build the final, stylishly elegant form. As French pâtisseries arrived in colonial America, they shared their culinary artistry with enthusiastic patrons, many of whom had experienced varieties of French pastry while traveling abroad. This dessert is best served the same day it is made, because the puff dough will get stale when sitting for too long.

1 recipe Puff Pastry (see page 201), or use
   store-bought sheets
Beaten egg whites, for brushing
Granulated sugar, for dusting
6 cups Pastry Cream (see page 202)
Confectioners' sugar, for dusting

1. Preheat the oven to 325°F.

2. Divide the puff pastry dough into three portions. Roll each portion into 1-inch-thick, roughly shaped rectangles about 6 × 12 inches. Prick each sheet of puff pastry with a fork, and transfer them to three separate parchment-lined baking pans.

3. Brush the tops of each sheet lightly with egg white and dust evenly with granulated sugar.

4. Bake for 15 minutes, or until golden brown. Let the pastry sheets cool; remove from the pans. Using a serrated knife, trim the pastry sheets to ensure they are exactly the same, squaring off corners and edges to align properly.

5. Spread about 1 tablespoon of pastry cream on the inverted side of a clean baking tray to act as "glue." Set one pastry sheet atop the baking tray, smooth side down. Spread an even 1-inch-thick layer of pastry cream on the first pastry sheet. Place the rough side of the second sheet directly on the cream. Chill the sandwiched layers for 20 minutes.

6. Spread an even 1-inch-thick layer of pastry cream atop the second sheet. Top with the third pastry layer, rough side down. Freeze for 20 minutes.

7. Sprinkle the top generously and evenly with confectioners' sugar. Chill 20 minutes, cut into eight portions, and serve.

CREAM PUFFS

MAKES APPROXIMATELY 12 (1-INCH) PUFFS

Cream puffs, luxurious combinations of delicate pastry and rich cream filling, are yet another type of confection that combines British and French baking traditions. Pastry cream has its roots in English pudding and custard preparation. Pâte à choux, however, also called "choux paste" and "cream-puff pastry," derives from French traditions. It translates as "cabbage paste," perhaps because as the dough rises in the oven it resembles little cabbages. William Verral shared a recipe for these delicacies in his 1759 *Complete System of Cookery*.

The cooks for the best families in eighteenth-century America would have had access to the latest books, including Verral's British work. He suggested filling the pastry with cherry conserve, much in the manner in which cream puffs are filled with pastry cream.

The recipe reads:

> [Y]our paſte make as follows; take half a pint of water, put to it a morſel of fine ſugar, a grain of ſalt and a bit of lemon-peel, an ounce of butter, and boil it a minute or two, take it from your fire, and work in as much fine flour as it takes to a tender paſte, put one egg at a time and mould it well till it comes to ſuch conſiſtence as to pour with the help of a ſpoon out of the ſtewpan upon a tin or cover, covered with flour; ſcrape it off in lumps upon tin with the handle of a large key, and bake them of a nice colour and criſpneſs, cut a hole in the bottom, and fill up with your conſerve, ſift ſome ſugar over, and diſh up. If you make this paſte according to the rule before you, it will ſwell very large and hollow, and makes a genteel "entremets."

Sweet tables at George Washington's Mount Vernon were often graced with a croquembouche (literally, "crunch in the mouth"), the towering centerpiece carefully assembled from cream puffs. Pastry chefs used caramel to cement the puffs together into a cone, drizzled hot caramel over the cone of pastry, and finished it with whimsical sugar sculptures.

1 recipe Pastry Cream (see page 202)

PÂTE À CHOUX

1 cup water
4 ounces (1 stick) unsalted butter
1½ teaspoons salt
¾ cup bread flour
3 eggs
1 egg yolk

1. Preheat the oven to 400°F and line two baking sheets with parchment paper.

2. In a medium-sized saucepan, bring the water, butter, and salt to a boil.

3. Remove the pot from the heat and add the flour all at once, stirring briskly to combine with a wooden spoon.

4. Return the mixture to the stove and cook over medium heat, stirring constantly, for 2 minutes.

5. Transfer the mixture to the bowl of an electric mixer. With the paddle attachment, mix the dough on low speed for 1 minute to cool slightly.

6. Raise the mixer to speed 2, add the eggs and yolk one at a time, beating until thoroughly combined between each addition. The dough should be smooth and relatively stiff.

7. Spoon the dough into a piping bag fitted with a medium straight tip (approximately ⅓-inch) and pipe it onto the lined baking sheets, forming twelve 1-inch domed rounds by applying firm, even pressure to the stationary bag, then ceasing pressure and swiftly sliding the bag forward and upward leaving no point on top of the round. (You can simply pat down any points with a wet fingertip to ensure perfect puffs).

8. Bake the dough at 400°F for 5 minutes, then reduce the temperature to 350°F and continue baking until deep golden brown and puffy, approximately 30 minutes. Keep the oven door closed as long as possible; the more air you let into the oven during the baking process, the less puffy the pastry will be.

9. Cool the puffs on a rack completely before filling or freezing.

10. Slice each puff in half, fill each half with pastry cream, and gently press them back together. Serve three puffs on a plate with warm chocolate sauce.

CHEF'S NOTE

When the eggs have all been added, remove the paddle, insert it 1 inch into the dough and pull it out, straight up, quickly. If the dough forms a relatively uniform V shape, it's ready to be piped. If it breaks off jaggedly, add the leftover egg white and mix until combined.

Drawing 1-inch circles, evenly spaced, on the reverse side of the parchment paper is an excellent piping guide.

VOL-AU-VENT WITH BERRIES

MAKES 6 SERVINGS

It is said that the esteemed gastronome and chef Marie-Antoine Carême first prepared the vol-au-vent. Carême worked in the kitchens of such renowned patrons as Talleyrand, Czar Alexander I, England's future George IV, and Baron James de Rothschild. In the invention of this dish, he elaborated on the late-eighteenth- and early-nineteenth-century English and French dishes that combined puff pastry with savory stews of meat or fish. The French term *vol au vent* means "flight in the wind," referring to the airiness of the pastry. It is delicious as he intended with stew or as it is here with a sweetened cream and topped with seasonal berries.

1 recipe Puff Pastry (see page 201), or use
   2 store-bought sheets
3 large eggs, beaten with 1 tablespoon water
   and pinch of salt, for egg wash
4 ounces semisweet chocolate

FILLING

1 pint heavy cream
¼ cup confectioners' sugar, plus extra for
   dusting
1 teaspoon vanilla extract
2 tablespoons orange liqueur, such as triple
   sec or Cointreau
1 pint each raspberries, blackberries,
   blueberries, and stemmed and halved
   strawberries
Fresh mint sprigs, for garnish

1. Preheat the oven to 425°F. Line an 11 × 17-inch baking pan with parchment paper.

2. Roll out one sheet of the puff pastry to ⅛-inch thickness and prick all over with a fork. Using a 4-inch biscuit cutter, cut the pastry into six rounds. Set these rounds aside; they will act as the base of the vol-au-vent.

3. Roll the other sheet of the puff pastry to ½-inch thickness and, using the same 4-inch cutter, cut six more rounds. Take a 3-inch biscuit cutter and cut the center out of each to create rings. Discard the 3-inch pieces or save for another use.

4. Brush the bases with the egg wash. Set the rings precisely atop the bases, making certain the edges are aligned. Brush each vol-au-vent with the egg wash, and refrigerate for 30 minutes.

5. Using a paring knife, make shallow cuts, ¼ inch apart, around the perimeter of each vol-au-vent. Brush each with egg wash again.

6. Place the pastries on the baking sheet. Transfer to the oven and bake for 20 minutes, or until golden. Remove from the oven, and set aside to cool.

7. Bring a medium-sized pot of water to a boil and turn it off. Place chocolate in a metal bowl and set it over the steaming pot of water. Stir occasionally until the chocolate is melted. Remove from the heat and let cool briefly. When cool enough to touch, using a pastry brush, paint the inside of the vol-au-vent with the melted chocolate.

8. Prepare the filling: In an electric mixer fitted with the whip attachment, whip the cream and confectioners' sugar on medium-high speed to medium peaks. Add the vanilla extract and orange liqueur, and whip to stiff peaks. Using a large spoon, fill each vol-au-vent with whipped cream and top with berries. Garnish with a fresh mint sprig.

DRIED CHERRY AND APRICOT TURNOVERS

MAKES 6 TURNOVERS

The morello cherry is a sweet-sour variety that makes dark juice and was very popular in plantains in the colonies. In her cookbook *The Art of Cookery Made Plain and Easy*, Hannah Glasse included a recipe for morello cherries preserved in sweet syrup. Adding copious amounts of sugar, vinegar, or alcohol to fruit and cooking it down would prevent the fruit from spoiling and make it possible to enjoy summer's harvest into the cold months.

TO BARREL MORELLO CHERRIES:

> To one pound of full ripe cherries picked from the ſtems, and wiped with a cloth, take half a pound of double refined ſugar, and boil it to a candy height, but not a high one; put the cherries into a ſmall barrel, then put in the ſugar by a ſpoonful at a time, till it is all in, and roll them about every day till they have done fermenting, then bung it up cloſe, and they will be fit for uſe in a month. It muſt be an iron-hooped barrel.

This recipe uses dried cherries, which would have come in handy for the eighteenth-century cook in the fall and winter months when fresh fruit was not available. Rather than making a traditional pie, bakers also made turnovers to add variety in size and shape to the sweet table. A table with multiple pies would not have been as visually interesting as one with a multitude of shapes. After all, one eats with the eyes before the mouth.

4 fresh apricots

1½ cups dried cherries

2 tablespoons (¼ stick) unsalted butter

1 tablespoon chopped fresh ginger

2 cups Apricot Preserves (see page 210)

2 tablespoons lavender honey, or regular honey

1 recipe puff pastry (see page XX), or use 2 store-bought sheets

3 large eggs, beaten with 1 tablespoon water and pinch of salt, for egg wash

½ cup granulated sugar

2 tablespoons ground ginger

1. Preheat the oven to 350°F. Line a baking pan with parchment paper.

2. Slice the apricots in half, remove the pits, and cut into 1-inch cubes. Place apricots in a medium-sized bowl, and add the cherries. Set aside.

3. In a medium-sized skillet, melt the butter over medium heat. Add the ginger and cook, stirring, for 30 seconds. Remove the skillet from the heat, and whisk in the apricot preserves and honey. Pour this mixture over the apricots and cherries; stir to combine.

4. Lightly dust your countertop with flour. With a lightly floured rolling pin, roll out the puff pastry to ¼-inch thickness. Trim the dough so that you have a 12 × 18-inch rectangle. Cut the sheet of pastry in half lengthwise, then cut each half into thirds.

5. Center one-sixth of the filling on each square.

6. Lightly brush the egg wash onto the pastry around the filling. Fold the pastry over the filling, corner to corner, to create a triangle. Seal the edges with a fork. Repeat the process for each square.

7. Evenly space the turnovers on the prepared baking pan, and make a small incision in the top of each turnover to vent. Brush the turnovers with the egg wash, and bake for 30 minutes.

8. Brush the turnovers with the egg wash again, and sprinkle with the sugar and ground ginger.

9. Bake the turnovers for another 5 to 10 minutes, or until golden. Serve warm.

QUINCE, CURRANT, AND DRIED FIG TURNOVERS

MAKES 6 TURNOVERS

Quince is related to apples and pears and is a fruit that never saw popularity in America as it did in Europe. It is not enjoyable eaten raw, as it has a thick skin and tannic flavor, but when cooked it makes an excellent jam or paste because the pulp turns pink and thickens.

As with many ingredients, first-generation settlers craved their taste of home, but as new generations took root, the fruit was less fashionable. Quince is available at some markets, but pears will make an acceptable substitute.

4 quince (or pears), peeled and cut into
   1-inch cubes
1 cup dried figs, chopped
½ cup currants or raisins
1 tablespoon lemon juice
2 ounces (½ stick) unsalted butter, melted
1 cup granulated sugar
¼ cup all-purpose flour
½ teaspoon cardamom
Freshly grated nutmeg to taste
1 recipe Puff Pastry (see page 201), or use
   2 store-bought sheets
6 tablespoons apple butter
1 egg beaten with 1 tablespoon of water,
   to be used as a wash
Light brown sugar, for sprinkling

1. Preheat the oven to 350°F. Line a baking pan with parchment paper.

2. Combine the quince, figs, currants or raisins, lemon juice, and the butter; toss to combine.

3. In a separate bowl, whisk together the sugar, flour, cardamom, and nutmeg. Add this mixture to the quince mixture, and stir to combine.

4. Lightly dust your countertop with flour. With a lightly floured rolling pin, roll out the puff pastry to ¼-inch thickness. Trim the dough so that you have a 12 × 18-inch rectangle. Cut the sheet of pastry in half lengthwise, then each half into thirds.

5. Place 1 tablespoon of the apple butter in the center of each square. The place one-sixth of the filling on each square and center it.

6. Lightly brush the egg wash on the pastry around the filling. Fold the pastry over the filling, corner to corner, to create a triangle. Seal the edges with a fork. Repeat the process for each square.

7. Evenly space the turnovers on the prepared baking pan, and make a small incision in the top of each turnover to vent. Brush the turnovers with the egg wash, and bake for 30 minutes.

8. Brush the turnovers with the egg wash again, and sprinkle with the brown sugar.

9. Bake the turnovers for another 5 to 10 minutes, or until golden. Serve warm.

STRUDEL

The crust of this pastry is a testament to the artistry of German and northern European baking traditions. The sweet fillings, however, rely on the bounty of American orchards. Strudel was, and can still be, prepared with items such as apples, cranberries, cherries, raspberries, peaches, apricots, berries, pears, raisins, citrus, and spices.

This strudel is sweet, crunchy, and comforting with its age-old combination of apples, raisins, and walnuts. Apples have been a favorite snack and healthy food item for centuries. Everyone knows that "An apple a day keeps the doctor away," but did you know that it was Benjamin Franklin who first wrote that? He so adored his American apples that he scolded his wife, Deborah, in a letter he wrote from London requesting very particular varieties of an apple:

> *"Goodeys I now and then get a few; but roasting Apples seldom, I wish you had sent me some; and I wonder how you, that used to think of everything, came to forget it. Newton Pippins would have been the most acceptable."*

Luckily, these heirloom varieties still exist and are available in farmers' markets in autumn during peak apple season. However, if you can't find two-hundred-year-old apple varieties in your local market, the standard baking apple of today will work with great success. Just don't tell Ben Franklin that you've cheated him on his Pippins.

DOUGH

2⅝ cups bread flour
1 egg
2 ounces (½ stick) unsalted butter
½ teaspoon salt
¾ cup warm water
1 cup canola oil

1. In the bowl of an electric mixer with the hook attachment, mix the bread flour, egg, butter, and salt until coarse crumbles form.

2. Add the water and mix for 15 minutes. The dough should be tacky but not sticky.

3. Pour the oil into a small bowl. Place the dough in the bowl, turn to coat with oil, so the dough does not dry out, cover, and refrigerate overnight. The dough will absorb some of the oil. Discard the leftover oil.

3 Granny Smith apples, cored and
    cut into 1-inch pieces
1 cup raisins
1 cup chopped walnuts
¾ cup sugar
1 tablespoon cinnamon
Pinch of grated nutmeg
2 tablespoons cake flour

Toss all ingredients together in a medium-sized bowl and set aside.

2 ounces (½ stick) unsalted butter, melted
¼ cup bread crumbs
1 egg white beaten with 1 tablespoon water,
    for egg wash
Granulated sugar, for sprinkling

1. Preheat the oven to 375°F.

2. Remove the dough from the bowl of oil and set on a cloth napkin to come to room temperature.

3. Lay a clean tablecloth, pillowcase, or bedsheet over a table or countertop, and dust heavily with all-purpose flour.

4. Place the dough ball in the center of the tablecloth and roll, using a rolling pin, outward in each direction, keeping the dough as rectangular as possible, until it is ½-inch thick. Let the dough rest.

5. Flour your hands and, from underneath, gently pull the dough lengthwise, using the backs of your hands, being careful not to tear the dough. Repeat in the other direction, stretching the dough until it is approximately 20 × 14 inches.

6. Brush the dough with the melted butter, sprinkle with the bread crumbs, then sprinkle the apple filling evenly over the dough, leaving 2 inches open at one side (to seal the log). Grasp the tablecloth under the section of the dough nearest you and pull it toward you, keeping the cloth only 2 inches above the filling, gathering the cloth and gently rolling the strudel until you've reached the bare 2 inches.

7. Brush the 2-inch strip with egg wash and roll the strudel on top, assuring that the seam remains on the bottom. Gently lift and curl the strudel onto a parchment-lined baking sheet in a U shape, then flatten and tuck the ends under. Brush with egg wash, sprinkle with sugar, and bake for 25 to 30 minutes or until golden and crisp.

Orange Curd-Filled Meringue Cup with Berries

MAKES 8 SERVINGS

Orange was always a popular choice on the sweet table, whether in curds, cakes, or creams. Mary Smith's 1772 recipe for orange ice cream in *The Complete House-keeper and Professed Cook*, a work "calculated for the greater ease and assistance of Ladies, House-keepers, Cooks, etc.," gave instructions to use oranges for an ice cream:

> Squeeze the juice of eight ſweet oranges in a bowl, add to it half a pint of water, and as much ſugar as will ſweeten it; ſtrain it through a ſieve, put it into an ice well, and freeze it 'till it is ſtiff; put it into a lead pine-apple mould, lap it well up in paper, put it into a pail of ice, and ſalt under and over it.

This recipe makes use of citrus by flavoring a curd that completes meringue and berries for an authentic eighteenth-century dessert that is welcome on any modern table.

MERINGUE

4 egg whites
1 cup granulated sugar
1 teaspoon cream of tartar

1. Preheat the oven to 200°F.

2. In the bowl of an electric mixer with the whisk attachment, whip the egg whites on medium speed until frothy.

3. In a small bowl stir together the sugar and cream of tartar, then add it to the egg whites as they whip, 2 tablespoons at a time.

4. Increase the speed to high and continue whipping until stiff peaks form.

5. Transfer the meringue to a piping bag fitted with a large star tip. Line a flat baking sheet with parchment paper or a silicon baking mat.

6. Pipe eight 2½-inch rounds, beginning in the center and working your way out.

7. To pipe the walls, pipe a circle on top of the outer edge of each round and continuously repeat another circle atop it. Then cease pressure while continuing the circular motion for a clean break. (Think of a coil.)

8. Bake for 2 hours at 200°F, then turn off the oven and allow to dry overnight. Do not open the oven door.

CHEF'S NOTE

Drawing the circles on the reverse side of the parchment (or on a sheet of parchment under a silicon baking mat) is an excellent piping guide.

ORANGE CURD

3 eggs

7 egg yolks

¾ cup granulated sugar

Zest of 1 orange

8 ounces fresh-squeezed orange juice

8 ounces (2 sticks) unsalted butter, cubed

1. In a stainless steel saucepan, whisk together the eggs, egg yolks, sugar, and orange zest until combined.

2. Whisk in the orange juice and cook over medium heat, stirring constantly, until the custard is very thick. When you drag a spatula along the bottom of the pot, you should be able to see the metal for a few seconds before the curd falls back on itself.

3. Remove the pot from the heat, pour the curd into a large bowl, and whisk in the butter.

4. Let stand, stirring occasionally, until the curd cools slightly.

5. Cover with plastic wrap, and chill until ready to serve.

6. Spoon chilled curd into each dried meringue cup and top with fresh berries.

CHAPTER 9

Ice Creams & Sorbets

FROZEN DESSERTS WERE AMONG THE MOST CELEBRATED OF EIGHTEENTH-CENTURY CONFECTIONS. BY THE LATE 1700S, FROZEN CREAMS AND FLAVORED ICES HAD ALREADY BEEN ENJOYED FOR CENTURIES, THEIR BEGINNINGS DATING BACK TO THE ANCIENT WORLD. ROMANS WERE KNOWN TO FINISH A MEAL WITH FROZEN DESSERTS SIMILAR TO SORBETS. DURING NERO'S REIGN OF ROME FROM 54 TO 68 BC, ICE WAS HARVESTED FROM NEARBY MOUNTAINS AND HELD IN "ICEHOUSES"—DEEP PITS COVERED WITH STRAW.

Centuries later, in England and France in the 1750s, these desserts gained popularity, as the aristocracy enjoyed them served in elegant glasses or elaborate molds. In prerevolutionary France, Louis XVI held dinners each Tuesday at Versailles where guests such as Thomas Jefferson ate ice cream. The royal family had delicate and ornate glasses designed specifically for eating ice cream. *Tasses à glace* made of costly European and Chinese porcelain were imported into America, but appeared only on the most well-to-do dining tables.

By the mid-eighteenth century, confectioners' shops in England, France, and even the American colonies were regularly serving ice cream and flavored ices. In 1790 the first ice cream parlor opened in New York. In late June 1791, a notice appeared in the *Pennsylvania Gazette* announcing the details of that year's July Fourth celebration. Among the entertainments to be featured at Grays Gardens were the confections of Mr. de la Croiz, including "iced creams of a great variety."

These treats were prized because of the arduousness of their preparation. Cooks made these dishes in several ways, all of which were time-consuming. Some recipes put the mixture in a tin set in a larger container of ice and salt. It was stirred occasionally until uniformly firm. Then, if desired, the ice cream or sorbet was placed in a mold and set again in the ice and salt until solid, which according to period recipes required about four hours. Hostesses served these treats in the shape of vegetables, fruits, and animals, thanks to special ice cream molds.

Not all ice creams were as sweet as we know them—recipes from England in the 1780s suggest making Parmesan ice cream and molding it to look like a wedge of cheese, complete with a rind made of caramelized sugar. Dolley Madison was well known for churning her favorite, oyster ice cream, in the early days of America.

All the hostesses of the day beamed with pride when the table was laden with ices and sweet creams. Join the founding mothers and serve fresh-churned homemade ice cream. It tastes much better than the styles available for purchase.

CHOCOLATE ICE CREAM

MAKES 1½ QUARTS

Like so many imports to the colonies, chocolate was weighted with politics. In protest of the British taxes on tea, ladies began having chocolate parties rather than tea parties. Coffeehouses sprang up and served hot sipping chocolate and coffee instead of tea.

During the Revolutionary War, both the American and British armies were given chocolate as part of their rations. At the time, chocolate was shipped in large, solid blocks, so it could be transported without spoiling. To make sure it remained affordable for the army, the Continental Congress imposed price controls on chocolate and cocoa in 1777. They made it illegal to export chocolate from Massachusetts, because it was necessary for the supply of the army.

4 cups heavy cream
½ cup granulated sugar, divided
8 ounces dark chocolate
3 egg yolks

1. Prepare an ice bath (see Chef's Note, page 85).

2. In a medium-sized saucepan, bring the cream, half of the sugar, and the chocolate to a simmer over low heat, stirring constantly.

3. Meanwhile, in a medium-sized bowl, whisk together the egg yolks and the remaining sugar until light.

4. Slowly add the hot cream to the egg mixture, ¼ cup at a time, whisking all the while.

5. Return the pot to the stove and cook over low heat, stirring constantly with a rubber spatula, until it is thick enough to coat the back of a spoon.

6. Transfer the custard to the ice bath and cool it, stirring occasionally, until it is cool to the touch. Remove from the ice bath, cover, and refrigerate until cold.

7. Spin in an ice cream maker, following the manufacturer's instructions.

Raspberry Sorbet

MAKES 1 QUART

Eighteenth-century cooks looked for creative ways to use the abundance of fruit picked from summer gardens. The most beautiful raspberries were likely preserved or eaten fresh and whole, while bruised berries were mashed and used for jams and frozen desserts. This sorbet's vibrant flavor relies on the freshest of ripe berries. When they are not in season, make this recipe with other berries.

George Washington is said to have spent $200 on equipment to make sorbet and ice cream on his estate. He owned several specialty ice cream pots made from tin and pewter. Unlike generic kitchen tins, this tool—a covered pail that was placed in a larger pail—was designed especially for preparing frozen desserts.

1 cup granulated sugar
¾ cup water
Juice and grated zest of 1 lemon
1 vanilla bean, split and seeds removed
2 cups raspberry puree, or frozen raspberries, thawed and pureed

1. In a small saucepan bring the sugar, water, lemon juice and zest, and vanilla seeds and pod to a boil.

2. Remove the pan from the heat, add the raspberry purée, and stir to combine. Transfer the sorbet base to a bowl, cover, and chill in the refrigerator until cold.

3. Remove the vanilla pod. Spin the sorbet base in an ice cream maker, following the manufacturer's instructions.

LEMON SORBET

MAKES 1½ QUARTS

Slightly tart but pleasantly sweet, this sorbet is lovely on its own or served with a tart or cookies. Lemons were prized for their flavor in desserts, and in more practical applications. Sea captains, including Captain James Cook, recorded their seeming ability to keep scurvy at bay.

Lemonade was popular all over Europe and in the colonies in the eighteenth century, as recipes for the thirst-quenching beverage traveled from France. British recipes suggested adding white wine to tart lemonade, and this sorbet would be equally well served with a splash of dessert wine before serving.

Describing Martha Washington's parties at Richmond Hill, New York, in July 1790, Abigail Adams wrote to her elder sister, Mary Cranch, that "she gives tea, coffee cake, lemonade & ice creams in summer."

3 cups water

1½ cups granulated sugar

1 tablespoon lemon zest

¾ cup lemon juice

¼ cup diced candied lemon peel

1. In a small saucepan, heat the water and sugar together until the sugar has dissolved.

2. Transfer the syrup to a bowl and stir in the zest and juice. Cover and refrigerate until cold.

3. Spin in an ice cream maker, following the manufacturer's instructions. Stir in candied lemon peel after spinning and before freezing.

CHESTNUT CREAM

MAKES 1½ QUARTS

No sweet table would have been complete without an ice cream dish. This "cream" uses an ingredient popular in the American colonies: chestnuts.

Modern recipes recommend scalding milk but not bringing it to a boil. Cooks in the eighteenth century probably relied on boiling as a method of pasteurization. Louis Pasteur invented the process of pasteurization, which uses heat to kill bacteria that cause liquids like milk and beer to spoil, in 1864. But because his ideas were revolutionary, they spread slowly. The idea of pasteurizing milk didn't arrive in the United States until the 1880s—and even then, it took more than thirty years to find wide acceptance.

2 cups heavy cream
2 cups half-and-half
½ cup granulated sugar
Pinch of salt
1 cup Glazed Chestnuts (see page 190), chopped

1. Stir together the cream, half-and-half, sugar, and salt until the sugar is dissolved.

2. Churn in an ice cream maker, following the manufacturer's instructions.

3. Stir in the chopped glazed chestnuts before freezing.

SAFFRON MOUSSE

MAKES 1 (1½-QUART) MOLD

Saffron adds a pretty, golden hue to a classic dessert. Pastry chef Emy published his treatise on ice creams *l'Art de bien faire les glaces d'office* in Paris in 1768 and described the importance of adding exotic ingredients to impress guests and add flavor to ices. He writes of ice creams flavored with liqueurs, chestnuts, coffee, and even saffron. Saffron was grown in Pennsylvania colonies as early as 1730, as Alsatian, German, and Dutch settlers came to the area and brought corms with them, carefully packed in trunks for the long voyage. High demand in the Caribbean made saffron literally worth its weight in gold. The trade's success ended in the wake of the War of 1812, when many merchant ships were destroyed. However, cuisine of that area still uses saffron, and it continues to grow in Lancaster, Pennsylvania.

2 cups heavy cream, divided

2 teaspoons saffron threads

2 egg whites

½ cup confectioners' sugar, divided

1 teaspoon vanilla, optional

1. In a small saucepan bring ½ cup of the heavy cream to a simmer. Stir in the saffron threads and allow to steep for 20 minutes. Mix with the remaining heavy cream in the bowl of an electric mixer; cover and place in refrigerator for 10 minutes.

2. In a separate medium-sized bowl, whip the egg whites until frothy. Gradually add ¼ cup of the sugar while whipping the whites to stiff peaks. Set aside.

3. Fit the mixing bowl of chilled cream into the mixer and whip it with the whisk attachment, gradually adding the remaining ¼ cup of sugar, just until soft peaks begin to appear.

4. Gently fold the stiff whites into the saffron cream, pour into an ice cream or gelatin mold, and freeze overnight.

5. The next day, invert the mold onto your serving plate, drape a hot moistened towel over the mold to loosen the mousse, remove the mold, and serve.

PARMESAN ICE CREAM

MAKES 1½ QUARTS

Frederick Nutt, whose *The Complete Confectioner* first appeared in 1789, gives thirty-two recipes for ice cream and twenty-four for water ices. He wrote a popular recipe for Parmesan ice cream that was churned, packed into a mold that looked like a wedge, and left to freeze. Once it was frozen, cooks removed the ice cream from the mold and decorated the back end with caramelized sugar to suggest a rind of cheese. The finished ice cream was a playful tease of its most flavorful ingredient as it looked like a giant wedge of aged cheese.

The original recipe reads "Take six eggs, half a pint of syrup and a pint of cream put them into stewpan and boil them until it begins to thicken; then rasp three ounces of parmesan cheese, mix."

4 cups heavy cream
½ cup granulated sugar, divided
1 cup finely grated Parmesan cheese
3 egg yolks

1. Prepare an ice bath (see Chef's Note, page 85).

2. In a medium-sized saucepan, bring the cream, half of the sugar, and the cheese to a simmer.

3. Meanwhile, in a medium-sized bowl, whisk together the egg yolks and remaining sugar until light.

4. Slowly add the hot cream to the egg mixture, ¼ cup at a time, whisking all the while.

5. Return the pot to the stove and cook over low heat, stirring constantly with a rubber spatula, until it is thick enough to coat the back of a spoon.

6. Transfer the custard to the ice bath and cool it, stirring occasionally, until it is cool to the touch. Remove from the ice bath, cover, and refrigerate until cold.

7. Spin in an ice cream maker, following the manufacturer's instructions.

8. Freeze for 30 minutes, or until firm enough to serve.

CHAPTER 10

Petits Fours & Sweetmeats

IN A CULINARY SENSE, PETITS FOURS MEANS SMALL BITES. THE TERM LITERALLY TRANSLATES FROM FRENCH AS "SMALL OVENS," MORE LOOSELY AS "SMALL BAKED GOODS." PETITS FOURS CAN BE EITHER SWEET OR SAVORY. THEY ARE OFTEN DAINTY LITTLE CAKES ORNAMENTED WITH ALL KINDS OF PRETTY PASTILLAGE, FONDANT, OR ICING. THE MOST COMMON PETITS FOURS ARE THE ONES THAT SPRING TO MIND—THE TINY SQUARE TEACAKES WITH LAYERS OF ICING COVERED IN FONDANT AND TOPPED WITH A COLORFUL FLOWER.

Think past those in the mind's eye. Stroll down a cobblestone street in eighteenth-century America past a bustling dry goods store, by a well-mannered tavern, and glimpse into a pastry shop's windows. You'll see lines of little uniform confections—all just large enough to make two bites.

Consider entertaining the city's loftiest residents and laying out a sweet table fit to impress even the dignitaries coming to dinner. The sweet table will need variety, color, and structure, and petits fours will be just the solution. The array could include macaroons, meringues, small éclairs, tartlets, candies, and sweetmeats. The term "sweetmeats" can be quite confusing also.

Throughout the eighteenth century, "sweetmeats" referred broadly to cakes, biscuits, cookies, and candied items such as fruit, seeds, flowers, and nuts (also known as comfits). It also included diverse dishes based on large quantities of sugar and fruit, including jellies and jams. Martha Washington, for example, recorded more than two hundred sweetmeat recipes in her cookery book. By the nineteenth century, the term was limited primarily to fruit cooked and preserved in sugar. In contrast to Washington's manuscript, Eliza Leslie's 1828 edition of *Seventy-Five Receipts, for Pastry, Cakes, and Sweetmeats* includes only sixteen sweetmeats, all of which are preserves, jams, or jellies.

MARZIPAN

MAKES 1½ POUNDS, OR ABOUT 20 PIECES

The European tradition of marzipan first appeared in fifteenth-century English texts as *march payne* and later as *marchpane*. Prepared with almonds, sugar, and rose or orange water, marzipan was one the most costly confections available in Europe. It was very popular in England, but didn't translate well into the colonies.

Two significant texts included March-pane or Marchpane recipes, however: Eliza Smith's *The Compleat Housewife* and Martha Washington's cookbook. Martha jotted down no fewer than five recipes. Like Smith, she called for shaping marzipan and then icing and baking it. These last two steps, essentially sugaring and drying, are usually omitted in modern versions.

Marzipan was primarily a confection of the wealthy. Not only were the ingredients expensive, but the colorful, fanciful shapes detailed in these recipes were primarily "conceits," whimsical, elegant sweetmeats meant as much to please the eye as the palate. Shining with gold leaf, sparkling with sugar, and decorated with dried fruit, marzipan was probably most enjoyed at dining tables laden with exotic foodstuffs, elaborate sugar figures, and fine wines.

1⅓ cups almond paste

5 tablespoons corn syrup

2 cups confectioners' sugar

3 tablespoons flavored liqueur of your choice (for example, applejack brandy if making marzipan apples)

¼ cup warm water

3 drops food coloring of your choice (for example, red if making apples)

1. In the bowl of an electric mixer fitted with the paddle attachment, beat together the almond paste and corn syrup on medium speed.

2. Sift the confectioners' sugar. With the mixer running on low speed, add the sugar in three intervals, incorporating each addition before adding the next.

3. Mix the marzipan until it is smooth. It will be stiff but should be malleable, the consistency of Silly Putty. Remove the marzipan from the bowl and knead in the liqueur by hand, 1 tablespoon at a time.

4. Shape the marzipan into whatever shape you desire, such as apples, and let them dry on a plate for 1 hour.

5. Stir together the water and food coloring, and paint the marzipan with a small pastry brush. To store, place the marzipan in a plastic storage container, lay plastic wrap directly on top of the marzipan, and cover with a tight-fitting lid.

Ganache Tartlets

MAKES 24 (1-INCH) TARTLETS

This petit four is always popular on the sweet table because it is so much more than just a bite of deeply flavored chocolate. The American love affair with cocoa and chocolate is as old as the nation itself, and indeed hails from an era much older than that. The first written records of chocolate in North America date as far back as the mid-seventeenth century when the Spaniards brought it with them from their tropical territories. By the time the thirteen colonies were established and on their way to becoming a nation of their own, chocolate was anchored in every man's diet.

Offering the highest quality chocolate became a point of pride to hosts and even to shop owners, who boasted the port of call where their chocolate originated. Before it was available in small bars or candies, chocolate was sold in large blocks. And it was not only an item of import, as some fastidious colonials began making their own chocolate by bringing in the cacao beans, roasting them, removing the husks, and crushing the beans by hand in large marble mortars with marble pestles. Benjamin Franklin advertised that he sold locally produced chocolate in his print shop in Philadelphia. In 1739 he was selling bibles and other books, pencils, ink, writing paper, and "very good chocolate."

½ recipe Pâte Sucrée (see page 200) rolled and baked into 1-inch tart shells, or use store-bought

½ cup Ganache (see page 205)

24 garnishes (toasted hazelnuts, candied orange peel, candied ginger, or the like)

1. Line up tart shells on a flat plate or baking sheet.

2. Spoon the warm ganache into the shells. When all the shells are full, give the tray a gentle tap to even out the ganache.

3. Chill the tartlets for 20 minutes, or until set. Top with a garnish of choice, and serve at room temperature.

Chocolate Bourbon Pecan Tartlets

MAKES 24 (1-INCH) TARTLETS

Although chocolate was fairly expensive in late-eighteenth-century America, it was widely available, sold in a variety of venues from dry goods stores to confectioners' shops.

Pecans are native to North and South America. Thomas Jefferson first cultivated pecan trees in his gardens at Monticello, and his passion for the "Poccon" or "Illinois nut," as it was called, was shared by George Washington, who planted trees at Mount Vernon. Jefferson, in fact, sent the general some pecan trees in January 1794 along with instructions concerning when to plant them. The sweet meat of the pecan was enjoyed by itself, candied and in cakes and tarts such as these.

1 egg

¼ cup granulated sugar

¼ cup light corn syrup

½ tablespoon melted unsalted butter

¼ teaspoon vanilla extract

Pinch of salt

1 tablespoon bourbon

1½ tablespoons grated semisweet or dark chocolate

½ recipe Pâte Sucrée (see page 200) rolled and baked into 1-inch tart shells, or use store-bought

½ cup chopped pecans

1. Preheat the oven to 300°F.

2. Whisk together the egg and sugar until they are light and frothy.

3. Whisk in all remaining ingredients except the pastry and pecans.

4. Line a baking sheet with parchment paper and space the tart shells evenly on it.

5. Fill each shell with 1 teaspoon chopped pecans, then spoon custard over the pecans until it nearly reaches the top.

6. Give the tray a gentle tap to even out the filling and bake for 5 to 10 minutes or until lightly puffed. Do not overbake, or the tartlets will become chewy and tough quickly.

GLAZED CHESTNUTS

MAKES 18 PIECES

Just like fruit, nuts were commonly preserved in the eighteenth century because they could spoil over time. Home cooks and confectioners cooked whole, shelled nuts in sugar syrup and, as with whole, unblemished fruit, stored them in jars to be served on the sweetmeat table or added to other dessert preparations. Among the nuts most frequently preserved during the period were walnuts and chestnuts, which grew on native trees. This sweetmeat is best served as an accompaniment to a dessert or as a decorative accent, but not on its own. Try it with chestnut pudding or chestnut ice cream.

18 fresh chestnuts (½ pound)
2 cups granulated sugar
1 cup honey
1 teaspoon cream of tartar
¼ cup light rum
1 pound confectioners' sugar

1. Bring a medium-sized saucepan of water to a boil. Prepare an ice bath (see Chef's Note, page 85) in a large stainless steel bowl.

2. Using a paring knife, slice an X in the flat side of the shell of each chestnut. Add 5 chestnuts at a time to the pot of boiling water, and cook for 1 minute. Using a slotted spoon, remove the nuts and set them on a dry kitchen towel. Carefully peel off the shells and papery skins with a paring knife while they're still hot. Let them cool.

3. In a medium-sized saucepan place 1 cup water. With a wooden spoon, stir in the sugar, honey, and cream of tartar. Wash down the sides of the pot with cool water and a pastry brush, making certain no sugar crystals remain. Bring the mixture to a boil; then remove the pot from the stove.

4. Add the chestnuts to the syrup, return the pan to medium heat, and cook until the mixture reaches a temperature of 260°F on a candy thermometer, 5 to 10 minutes. Set the pot in the ice bath, and allow to cool to room temperature.

5. Transfer the mixture to a plastic container. With a wooden spoon, stir in the rum. Cover and refrigerate the chestnuts in the syrup for 2 days in order to allow them to absorb the syrup.

6. Strain the chestnuts and set them atop a wire rack to dry at room temperature for 30 minutes.

7. Meanwhile, in a small bowl, stir the confectioners' sugar with ¼ cup water until a paste the consistency of yogurt is formed. Pour the glaze over the chestnuts to coat each evenly and completely. Serve immediately or store covered in the refrigerator for up to 4 days.

Candied Ginger

MAKES 4 CUPS

Cooks used ginger in savory and sweet dishes. Candying it became a popular way to preserve this flavorful root and to tame its fiery bite. There are many ways to candy ginger, but Martha Washington wrote a recipe that more closely resembles the process of candying nuts: she coated them with hard sugar. Martha instructed that the ginger be soaked in water overnight. Sugar was then to be boiled and cooled and the ginger added to it, stirring until the lot was "hard to ye pan." The ginger was removed, dried, and placed again in a hot pan, where, as it cooled, the cook was to "stir it about roundly, and it will be A rock Candy in A very short space."

The following recipe marries both techniques, resulting in a sweetmeat that is translucent, tender, and coated with sugar.

1 pound fresh ginger, peeled
10 cups granulated sugar, divided

1. Place the ginger in a medium-sized saucepan, and add enough cold water to cover completely. Place the pan over high heat and bring the mixture to a boil. Immediately remove from the heat, strain, and rinse the ginger under cool running water. Allow the ginger to cool to room temperature.

2. Using a mandoline, or carefully with a chef's knife, slice the cooled ginger into ¼-inch-thick slices. Place the slices in a pot and cover with cold water. Bring to a boil. Strain and rinse the sliced ginger under cool running water. Repeat the boiling, straining, and rinsing process four more times to remove the bitterness from the ginger.

3. In a medium-sized pot, place the sliced ginger, 6 cups of the sugar, and 4 cups water; stir to combine. Using cool water and a pastry brush, wash down the sides of the pot, making certain no sugar crystals remain. Bring the mixture to a boil and cook until the syrup reaches a temperature of 260°F on a candy thermometer, about 10 minutes. Remove the pot from the heat and allow it to cool to room temperature. Cover the pot with plastic wrap, and let the ginger steep overnight at room temperature.

4. Strain the slices from the syrup and arrange them atop a wire rack. Cover generously with 2 cups of the sugar. Turn the ginger slices over, and repeat the process with the remaining 2 cups of sugar.

5. Let the sugar-coated ginger sit out for 8 hours. Store in an airtight container for up to 3 weeks at room temperature or frozen in freezer bags for up to 6 months.

POACHED PEARS

MAKES 4 SERVINGS

Eighteenth-century Philadelphia belle Nancy Shippen often mentioned sweetmeat preparation in her journal. In 1783 she noted: "I spent a most agreeable evening though a large company, which is seldom the case a most admirable supper, excellent wine an elegant desert of preservd fruits & every body in spirits good humor. It is now late & I am sleepy." In late summer 1784 she wrote, "I spent the day at home very busy making sweet-meets for the winter." And again on Monday, September 13, 1784, she commented, "This day employd as usual in domestic affairs, serving peaches &c."

This recipe for poached pears is probably very similar to one Nancy Shippen would have prepared for her family's guests in the autumn.

3 cups Merlot wine

¾ cup granulated sugar

2 cinnamon sticks

1 tablespoon whole cloves

1 vanilla bean

4 underripe Bartlett pears, peeled and cored, but left whole

1. In a large stainless steel or enameled saucepan, combine the wine, sugar, cinnamon sticks, cloves, and vanilla bean. Bring to a boil, then reduce the heat to a simmer.

2. Add the pears to the pan. To make sure they are evenly submerged in the liquid, weight them down with a heat-safe plate. Simmer, covered, until the pears are fork tender, about 15 minutes. Do not overcook.

3. Meanwhile, fill a large bowl with ice water.

4. With a slotted spoon, carefully remove the pears from the pan and immediately transfer them to the ice water. Once cooled, return the cooled fruit to the cooled poaching liquid and store, covered and refrigerated, for up to 3 days.

CANDIED PECANS

MAKES 12 SERVINGS

This recipe was inspired by the many candied fruits, flowers, and even spices prepared in eighteenth-century homes and confectioners' shops. Today, dried nuts of many varieties are readily available and quite common. In the American colonies during the mid- to late 1700s, however, sugar and nuts were costly and enjoyed sparingly. These sweet, crunchy pecans are delicious enjoyed on their own as a traditional sweetmeat or as a topping for ice cream.

1 egg white
½ cup granulated sugar
1 teaspoon freshly grated nutmeg
1 teaspoon ground cinnamon
½ teaspoon salt
3 cups pecans

1. Preheat the oven to 300°F.

2. Line a baking sheet with parchment paper.

3. In the bowl of an electric mixer, whisk the egg white until foamy.

4. Add the sugar, spices, and salt and whisk until the mixture is thick and opaque.

5. Fold in the pecans until coated. Transfer to the baking sheet with a fork, leaving space between them.

6. Bake until deep golden brown, about 30 minutes. Cool completely on the sheet, then transfer to an airtight container and store at room temperature.

Spiced Candied Walnuts

MAKES 16 SERVINGS

Black walnuts grow naturally in northeastern North America, and Native Americans such as the Lenapes, whose territory ran along the Delaware River, ate the fruit from the tree well before settlers arrived. As Europeans came to the colonies, they transported English walnuts to New England, making both nuts available and an excellent source of protein and flavor in the diet. Black walnuts are smaller, harder to pick, and less abundant, so the European varieties quickly grew more popular. This recipe is similar to making a spiced meringue, and then adding nuts before baking. The nuts roast as the clusters turn beige from the egg whites browning.

1 large egg white
½ cup granulated sugar
1 teaspoon nutmeg, freshly grated
1 teaspoon ground cinnamon
½ teaspoon ground clove
½ teaspoon ground ginger
½ teaspoon salt
4 cups whole walnuts

1. Preheat the oven to 300°F. Line a baking sheet with parchment paper and lightly coat it with nonstick spray.

2. In the bowl of an electric mixer with the whisk attachment, whip the egg white until foamy. Gradually add the sugar, increasing the speed of the mixer until all the sugar is incorporated.

3. Add the spices and whip until the mixture is stiff and opaque, 3 to 5 minutes.

4. Stir in the nuts with a spatula to coat, then spoon them onto the prepared sheet tray and separate them with a fork.

5. Bake until golden brown, approximately 30 minutes, and allow to cool completely on the baking sheet.

6. Store in an airtight container at room temperature for up to 4 days.

Diablotins or Little Devils

MAKES APPROXIMATELY 24 QUARTER-SIZED PIECES

Before candy bars and cooking chocolate were available for purchase, cooks had to pound cacao beans into a powder with a large mortar and pestle, and then add oil or butter to form chocolate as we know it today. A popular French recipe in the 1750s for this chocolate treat suggests cooks should use "chocolate pounded, made malleable with some good oil, and formed into a hard paste." Today's cooks can use chocolate pieces, so much of the work has been removed from this recipe. In the past, cooks might form the chocolate to look like walnuts or olives, or leave it flat and allow sugared cinnamon, colorful nonpareils, or nuts to stick out, in an early version of today's popular chocolate bark. This treat has endless possibilities. Make diablotins with any type of chocolate, nuts, and candied fruits in any combinations, just use the same proportions listed below.

16 ounces dark chocolate
1 cup toasted, slivered almonds
½ cup finely chopped crystallized ginger
½ cup dried cranberries

1. Melt the chocolate slowly over a double boiler, or in the microwave in 15-second intervals.

2. Stir in almonds, ginger, and cranberries.

3. Spoon out, in quarter-sized clusters, onto a parchment-lined baking sheet

4. Refrigerate until set.

CHAPTER 11

Crusts & Complements

THIS CHAPTER IS CHOCK-FULL OF THE VERY LESSONS THAT MRS. GOODFELLOW WOULD HAVE BESTOWED UPON HER PUPILS. HERE YOU WILL FIND THE ESSENTIALS TO FINE CAKES, PIES, PASTRIES, AND SWEETS. THESE ARE THE BUILDING BLOCKS. IN ORDER TO CREATE AN IDEAL PIE OR TART, YOU MUST START AT THE VERY FOUNDATION—THE CRUST. WHEN THE RECIPE CALLS FOR A SPECIFIC CRUST, YOU WILL FIND DETAILED DIRECTIONS IN THIS SECTION.

Likewise, some of the tarts call for jam. Eighteenth-century cooks would not have been able to go to the grocer's for ingredients, but they would have the know-how to create these most basic elements. Preserves, chutneys, and jams would have required quite a bit of attention. The fruit had to be stemmed and washed, and the fire stoked; once the ingredients were combined, the sweetened fruit demanded a constant and watchful eye until it reached just the right consistency—a difficult task when the fire was roaring and other dishes had to be cooked. There were no ready-made sauces or foods, so a cook might be removing feathers from a freshly slaughtered hen while making jam,

baking bread, simmering the supper's stew, and managing a staff.

Most of the "receipts" or recipes from the era assume that a cook has years of experience in front of the hearth and has grown up learning the tricks of the trade. The housewives of the era were well trained from the early years in developing frugal and functional ways to make use of every last morsel of food and make it delicious and hearty.

Hannah Glasse instructs her readers to "use a good crust" in a "pye." She gives instructions for no fewer than nine versions, including a dripping crust, a standing crust, a crust for custards, and two crusts for tarts. In her 1764 book *English Housewifry*, Elizabeth Moxon tells her readers that in making apricot custard "if it be at the time that you have no ripe apricots, you may lie preserved apricots." This makes the assumption that any cook would know how to make apricot preserves and have them handy in the cupboard. Her book's long subtitle goes on to describe it as "A Book necessary for Mistresses of Families, higher and lower Women Servants, and confined to Things USEFUL, SUBSTANTIAL and SPLENDID."

Because not all modern cooks have been so well versed with years in the kitchen lore, we break down the steps and give you recipes to make your own. Rather than use store-bought elements, try the authentic and historical method of doing it yourself. These pages contain the very best recipes for crusts, jams, pastry creams, and other necessary building blocks to turn out perfect desserts.

PÂTE BRISÉE

MAKES 1 (9-INCH) PIE CRUST

This piecrust is more versatile than its sweet sister, pâte sucrée. It is ideal for both sweet and savory tarts and pies and is as much at home in a quiche as in an apple pie. It prevents a fruit or custard pie from being too sweet and creates the best base for most pies. As with most crusts, though, the devil is in the details. Be sure to use cold ingredients and don't overmix the dough. Many modern recipes claim that the dough will turn out just as well when made in a food processor or mixer, but for best results, stick with the centuries-old French method of making it by hand and rolling it out.

1⅔ cups sifted all-purpose flour

¼ teaspoon salt

4 ounces (1 stick) cold unsalted butter, cubed

4–5 tablespoons ice water

1. In a medium-sized bowl, stir together flour and salt.

2. Using a pastry cutter, or your hands, cut in the cold butter until the mixture is a course crumble.

3. Sprinkle in water 1 tablespoon at a time and toss together until a dough ball starts to form. Add only enough water to hold the ball together.

4. Form the dough into a disc, wrap tightly in plastic wrap, and refrigerate for at least 30 minutes before use.

5. When ready to use, preheat an oven to 400°F.

6. Roll out the dough on a floured surface into a round about ¼-inch thick.

7. If the crust is to be prebaked, line the pie dough with aluminum foil or parchment paper and gently pour in dried beans or rice to weight down the dough and prevent it from buckling in the pan. Bake 15 minutes, or until golden brown.

CHEF'S NOTE

Carefully follow the instructions for each pie recipe. Some recipes instruct cooks to bake the dough before filling it, while others combine the raw filling with the raw dough and bake together.

PÂTE SUCRÉE

MAKES 1 (9-INCH) DOUBLE-CRUST PIE, OR 2 (9-INCH) ROUND PIE CRUSTS

This is the sweet, crumbly dough most often used in tarts for a sturdy, tender base. It is the most basic of French pastry techniques that early Americans imported from the palaces and simple bake shops of Paris. Dignitaries such as Thomas Jefferson would have sampled the buttery, flaky crusts in tarts completed with custards, creams, or fruit when traveling abroad. When it's made well, pâte sucrée has the crumbly texture of shortbread cookies and yet can support the heaviest filling without cracking to pieces. For best results, avoid the temptation to speed up the process by using modern-day mixers, and make this dough by hand with the coldest ingredients possible. Dough can be made up to two weeks ahead of time, stored in the freezer, and thawed overnight in the refrigerator before using, keeping it cold at all times.

3 cups sifted all-purpose flour

⅓ cup granulated sugar

½ teaspoon salt

8 ounces (2 sticks) cold unsalted butter, cubed

2 large eggs

1. In a medium-sized bowl, stir together the flour, sugar, and salt.

2. Using a pastry cutter, or your hands, cut in the cold butter until the mixture is a course crumble.

3. Add the eggs and mix until a dough ball forms, being careful not to overmix the dough.

4. Form the dough into a disc, wrap tightly in plastic wrap, and refrigerate for at least 30 minutes before use.

5. When ready to use, preheat an oven to 400°F.

6. Roll out the dough on a floured surface into a round about ¼-inch thick.

7. If the crust is to be prebaked, line the pie dough with aluminum foil or parchment paper and gently pour in dried beans or rice to weight down the dough and prevent the dough from buckling in the pan. Bake 15 minutes, or until golden brown.

CHEF'S NOTE

Carefully follow the instructions for each pie recipe. Some recipes instruct cooks to bake the dough before filling it, while others combine the raw filling with the raw dough and bake together.

PUFF PASTRY

MAKES 2 (12 X 8-INCH) SHEETS

Preparing traditional puff pastry is a rewarding and worthwhile but time-consuming task that requires several hours of work. Chilled butter and a flour-and-water mixture are rolled and folded together in thirds at least six times, creating hundreds of delicate layers that expand during baking. The process is a long one, because the pastry must remain very cold and rest in the refrigerator in between turns (the term for the rolling and folding procedure). As a time-saving alternative, high-quality, frozen puff pastry is available in supermarkets as well.

2¾ cups plus 2 tablespoons bread flour, divided

1 cup pastry flour

1 tablespoon salt

1 cup very cold water

1 pound (4 sticks) unsalted butter

1. Reserve ½ cup of the bread flour for later. In the bowl of an electric mixer fitted with the dough hook, combine the rest of the bread flour (2¼ cups plus 2 tablespoons), the pastry flour, and the salt. Add the ice water and mix on medium-slow speed until a smooth dough forms.

2. Remove the dough from the bowl and roll it out into a 10 × 16-inch rectangle. Place on a floured baking sheet, wrap in plastic, and refrigerate for 30 minutes.

3. Clean the bowl and then mix the remaining ½ cup of bread flour and the butter with the paddle attachment until smooth. Do not whip.

4. Coat a work surface generously with flour. Lay out the chilled dough and spread the butter mixture on top of the dough, covering the left-hand two-thirds of dough, and leaving a 1-inch border of dough uncovered around the edges.

5. Fold the unbuttered right-hand third of the dough over, from right to left; then fold the butter-covered third over, from left to right. Seal all of the edges so that no butter is showing.

6. Turn the dough so that the seam is facing away from you; then, using a rolling pin, roll the dough out to 24 × 16 inches. Fold the dough again, using the same method as used when folding in the butter. Place the dough back onto the baking sheet, cover with plastic wrap, and refrigerate for an additional 30 minutes.

7. Coat a work surface generously with flour. Lay out the chilled dough so the seam is facing away from you. Using a rolling pin, roll the dough out to 24 × 16 inches again. Fold the left-hand quarter of the dough in, and then fold the right-hand quarter of the dough in, so that the edges touch in the middle. Then fold the two halves together as if closing a book.

8. Cover with plastic wrap, and refrigerate for 30 minutes.

9. Repeat step 7; then cover and refrigerate for another 30 minutes.

10. Repeat step 7 again; then cover and refrigerate for another 30 minutes.

11. Repeat step 7 yet again; then cover and refrigerate for 1 hour before use. The puff pastry will last 3 to 4 days in the refrigerator but can be frozen for up to 1 month and defrosted 1 day before use.

PASTRY CREAM

MAKES APPROXIMATELY 2½ CUPS

The custard called pastry cream is one of the most basic and versatile elements of pastry. It may have been known as *crème pâtissière* to cooks in the eighteenth century who wanted to replicate stylish French desserts. It is just as delectable today as it was then and can be used for pies, pastries, trifles, and much more.

2 cups whole milk
½ cup granulated sugar, divided
1 egg
2 egg yolks
5 tablespoons cornstarch, sifted
2 tablespoons unsalted butter
1½ teaspoons vanilla extract (or flavoring of choice)

1. Set out a 9 × 13-inch glass or ceramic casserole dish.

2. In a small saucepan, heat the milk and ¼ cup of the sugar to a simmer.

3. While the milk is heating, in a medium-sized bowl whisk together the egg, yolks, remaining ¼ cup sugar, and cornstarch until smooth.

4. Once the milk has simmered, add it, ½ cup at a time, to the egg mixture, whisking all the while, until it has been completely incorporated.

5. Return the mixture to the pot and cook over low heat, stirring constantly with a rubber spatula, until the mixture begins to thicken.

6. Pay close attention to the thickening mixture, and when the first boiling bubble comes through, remove the pan from the heat and whisk in the butter and vanilla.

7. Immediately pour the custard into the casserole dish, spread it evenly, and lay plastic wrap directly on the surface.

8. Refrigerate until the custard has cooled completely.

Crème Anglaise

The French term *crème anglaise* has stuck in American kitchens over the centuries. This custard is much softer than its cousin pastry cream and is commonly served poured over desserts. Originally the sweet sauce evolved from the kitchens of ancient Romans who used eggs as thickeners to create custards and creams. This is a basic recipe and can be flavored with your choice of liqueurs or extracts, or you can steep spices or citrus peels in the cream before mixing.

1 cup heavy cream
1 egg yolk
3 tablespoons granulated sugar
2 tablespoons liqueur, optional
1 teaspoon vanilla or almond extract, optional

1. Prepare an ice bath (see Chef's Note, page 85). In a small saucepan bring the heavy cream to a simmer over medium heat.

2. In a small bowl, whisk together the egg yolk and sugar until lightened.

3. Carefully whisk the hot cream into the yolk, ¼ cup at a time. If using, add the liqueur and vanilla or almond extract.

4. Return the mixture to the pot and cook, stirring constantly, over low heat until the custard thickens enough to coat the back of a spoon.

5. Pour into a small bowl and chill over the ice bath, stirring occasionally until cool.

Syllabub

MAKES 6 SERVINGS

Every eighteenth-century sweet table would have been graced with a syllabub, and many twenty-first-century tables are, too. These sweetened, seasoned creams could be considered the grandmother of the milk shakes and café drinks served today. There are primitive recipes stretching from the first settlers in America and more sophisticated versions that call for imported wines and extracts to add flavor. A recipe from the early years recorded by the Salem Moravians reads "Take one pint of wine, sweeten it pretty sweet with loaf sugar, grate half a nutmeg in it, and then milk the cow in the wine." This recipe can be enjoyed with a spoon, although it is lighter than puddings or creams.

2½ cups heavy cream
1 cup sugar
1 lemon, zested and juiced
1 cup white wine, such as Riesling
¼ cup brandy
¼ cup sherry

1. Whip the cream with an electric mixer until frothy. Slowly add sugar as it whips, until light and frothy.

2. Turn mixer to low speed and add lemon zest and juice, wine, brandy, and sherry.

3. Pour the syllabub into wine glasses or dessert glasses and let chill overnight to allow flavors to marry. Serve chilled.

GANACHE

This chocolatey treat is wonderful as an icing, filling, glaze, or sauce. While ganache can be made with white, dark, or milk chocolate, and flavorings can be added, this version is a classic, simple and very rich recipe.

It is delicious on any style of cake but it is a decadent addition to Martha Washington's mousse and chocolate layer cake.

2 cups heavy cream
2 cups dark chocolate, coarsely chopped

1. Measure out chocolate into a metal or glass bowl.

2. Bring cream to a simmer in a saucepot, stirring once or twice to ensure the bottom doesn't burn.

3. Pour hot cream over chocolate and let rest for 1 minute.

4. Beginning with small circles in the center, stir cream and chocolate together with a rubber spatula or wooden spoon until it starts to come together, then move outward until the cream and chocolate are completely homogenized. Ganache will be warm and ready to pour onto cake or use in recipes.

Vanilla Sponge Cake

MAKES 1 (10-INCH) ROUND

Recipes for sponge cake appear in many period cookbooks under that title as well as under "biscuit de savoye" or "biscuit de savoie," which means Savoy sponge. Thomas Jefferson's recipe collection identifies one that he preferred his cooks to use. As it is today, the sponge cake was prized for its light, delicate texture. This is achieved by combining its ingredients in a particular method. Eighteenth-century cookbook authors laid it out very clearly for their readers and recommended they follow the steps closely.

Use this versatile cake recipe to build a lovely trifle, or ice it with one of the many options in the book. It would be just as delicious with a simple sugar meringue icing, like the one given with Martha Washington's Great Cake (see page 47), as it would be with the orange buttercream icing that complements Martha Washington's Excellent Cake.

3½ cups plus 3 tablespoons granulated sugar, divided

8 egg yolks

⅔ cup vegetable oil

1 cup cold water

1 tablespoon vanilla extract

3½ cups cake flour

1 tablespoon plus 1 teaspoon baking powder

1 teaspoon salt

8 egg whites

1. Preheat the oven to 325°F. Grease a 10-inch cake pan and line it with parchment.

2. Reserve 1 cup plus 1 tablespoon sugar for later. In the bowl of an electric mixer with the whip attachment, whisk together the rest of the sugar (2½ cups plus 2 tablespoons) and the egg yolks until light and fluffy.

3. Stream in the oil, then the cold water and the vanilla extract.

4. Turn off the mixer, add the dry ingredients, and mix on low speed until moistened. Turn the mixer to high and whip for 30 seconds. Set this mixture aside.

5. Clean and carefully dry the whip attachment of the mixer. In a clean, dry bowl, whip the egg whites until foamy. Add the reserved sugar, 2 tablespoons at a time, and whip to stiff peaks.

6. Gently fold the egg whites into the larger mixture, pour into the prepared cake pan, and bake for 45 minutes to 1 hour or until a toothpick inserted comes out clean or with dry crumbs.

7. Cool in the pan on a wire rack for 15 minutes, then turn out and cool completely.

Raspberry Shrub

MAKES 4 CUPS

Shrub can be made with just about any berry or fruit. It was an early method of preserving the seasonal harvest. Although scientists had not discovered bacteria yet, cooks figured out that mold and other harmful growth did not occur in food with high sugar or vinegar content. Today, cooks may not need to make it to preserve fruits, but it adds a sweet zing to recipes, whether used in salad dressings, drizzled over ice cream, or combined with Champagne for a cocktail.

1 cup sugar

1 cup water

2 pints raspberries

2 cups white wine vinegar

1. In a medium saucepan, whisk together the sugar and water, and bring to a boil over high heat, stirring occasionally. Reduce the heat to medium and cook 3 to 5 minutes. The syrup should not take on any color.

2. Wash the raspberries well and add to the syrup. Cook, stirring occasionally, until the raspberries are completely cooked down, about 8 to 10 minutes.

3. Pour in the vinegar, bring to a boil, and cook for 2 minutes.

4. Remove from heat and strain through cheesecloth or a fine mesh sieve. Cool to room temperature and store, refrigerated, in an airtight container for up to 6 months.

BERRY PRESERVES

MAKES 2 CUPS

Certainly the expense of preserves added to the panache associated with them, because fresh fruit was still a luxury and sugar was costly. In a 1780 letter, a visitor to Mount Vernon remarked little on most of the dishes served at dinner but expounded upon the elegant preserves the Washingtons offered:

> I paid no attention to them [all of the dishes] as I was restricted to a severe diet and they have escaped from my memory. I can only say that I saw there for the first time preserved strawberries whether that kind of sweetmeats was then not so common in France as in this country or whatever may be the cause, I had never seen any before. Those were very large and beautiful, and I indulged in eating a few of them. I have been very fond of them ever since.

2 pints berries, such as blackberries, raspberries, strawberries, gooseberries, or blueberries

2 cups granulated sugar

¾ cup water

1 tablespoon freshly squeezed lemon juice

1. Prepare an ice bath (see Chef's Note, page 85).

2. Place the berries in a strainer and rinse with cold water. Pat the berries dry with a paper towel.

3. Choose a saucepan large enough to hold three times the amount of ingredients being used. Place in it the sugar, water, and lemon juice; stir to combine. Wash down the sides of the pot with cool water and a pastry brush, making certain no sugar crystals remain. Bring the sugar syrup to a boil over high heat, washing down the sides of the pot often. Cook the syrup until it reaches a temperature of 285°F on a candy thermometer.

4. Remove from the heat. Carefully add a few berries at a time. The mixture will spatter, so add the berries slowly, close to the syrup, stirring constantly. Once all of the berries have been added, return the saucepan to the heat, and continue to stir the mixture until it returns to a boil. Reduce the heat to medium and cook until the mixture is thickened, 8 to 10 minutes.

5. Once the preserves have reached the desired thickness, transfer them to a stainless steel bowl and set the bowl in the ice bath to cool to room temperature (see Chef's Note, page 85).

6. Store the preserves in an airtight container in the refrigerator for up to 2 weeks.

APRICOT PRESERVES

MAKES 2 CUPS

Preserves and jams were considered sweetmeats and were among the most elegant served on the sweet table. Whether prepared with imported fruits and spices or with ingredients from local gardens, these dishes were always admired and celebrated. Sugar was costly in the eighteenth century, so preserved fruit was expensive to produce.

When a hostess presented a dessert table of preserved fruits, her guests would have implicitly understood and appreciated the high level of hospitality to which they were being treated. Likewise, guests will appreciate the great care that jams and preserves require because in today's hectic world, many cooks rarely find the time to make their own preserves, so you may get a similar reaction.

8 apricots

1½ cup granulated sugar

½ cup water

¼ cup honey

1 tablespoon freshly squeezed lemon juice

2 tablespoons rose water

1. Bring a medium-sized saucepan of water to a boil. Fill a large bowl with ice water.

2. Wash the ripe fruit well. Slice the fruit in half and remove the pits. Cook the apricots in the boiling water until fork tender, about 3 minutes. Remove them from the pot and immediately submerge them in the ice water. Peel off the skin with a paring knife. Pat the apricots dry with a paper towel.

3. Transfer the fruit to a food processor and puree. You should have about 2 cups of puree.

4. Choose a saucepan large enough to hold three times the amount of ingredients being used. Place in it the sugar, water, honey, and lemon juice; stir to combine. Wash down the sides of the pot with cool water and a pastry brush, making certain no sugar crystals remain. Bring the sugar syrup to a boil over high heat, washing down the sides of the pot often. Cook the syrup until it reaches a temperature of 285°F on a candy thermometer.

5. Remove from the heat. Carefully stir the fruit puree into the sugar syrup. The mixture will spatter, so add it slowly, close to the syrup, stirring constantly. Once all of the pulp has been added, return the saucepan to the heat and continue to stir the mixture until it returns to a boil. Reduce the heat to medium-high and cook until the mixture is thickened.

6. While it is cooking, prepare an ice bath (see Chef's Note, page 85). Once the preserves have reached the desired thickness, stir in the rose water. Transfer the preserves to a stainless steel bowl placed in the ice bath, and cool to room temperature.

7. Store the preserves in an airtight container in the refrigerator for up to 2 weeks.

Apple, Pear, or Quince Wine Preserves

MAKES 2 CUPS

Madeira was extremely popular in the American colonies, but known to the British as the poor man's drink. Treaties with Portugal allowed British merchants to import it without paying taxes, so it was affordable. What the Americans found, however, is that the journey in the holds of ships enriched the wine. Madeira jostled in oak barrels, absorbed seawater and rain water, and aged on its long journey to the Americas, making it luscious and economical.

5 apples (Gala or Granny Smith), 5 pears, or 5 quinces
1¾ cups granulated sugar
½ cup honey
½ cup Madeira wine
½ cup water
2 teaspoons cider vinegar

1. Bring a medium-sized saucepan of water to a boil. Fill a large bowl with ice water.

2. Wash the fruit well. Peel the fruit and slice it in half. Remove the cores. Cook the fruit in the boiling water until fork tender, about 3 minutes. Remove the fruit from the pot and immediately submerge it in the ice water. Pat the fruit dry with a paper towel.

3. Transfer the fruit to a food processor and puree. You should have about 2 cups of fruit puree.

4. Choose a saucepan large enough to hold three times the amount of ingredients being used. Place in it the sugar, honey, wine, water, and vinegar; stir to combine. Wash down the sides of the pot with cool water and a pastry brush, making certain no sugar crystals remain. Bring the sugar syrup to a boil over high heat, washing down the sides of the pot often. Cook the syrup until it reaches a temperature of 285°F on a candy thermometer.

5. Remove from the heat. Carefully add fruit puree a bit at a time. The mixture will spatter, so add the puree slowly, close to the syrup, stirring constantly. Once all of the puree has been added, return the saucepan to the heat and continue to stir the mixture until it returns to a boil. Reduce the heat to medium and cook until the mixture is thickened, 8 to 10 minutes.

6. While it is cooking, prepare an ice bath (see Chef's Note, page 85). Once the preserves have reached the desired thickness, transfer them to a stainless steel bowl set in the ice bath, and cool to room temperature.

7. Store the preserves in an airtight container in the refrigerator for up to 2 weeks.

ORANGE MARMALADE

MAKES 2 CUPS

Many cookbooks of the era devoted entire chapters to preserves and marmalades. John Farley in *The London Art of Cookery* offered readers "Preliminary Hints and Observations" that advised paying particular attention to storing them when finished. It would defeat the purpose of making preserves if the expensive fruit spoiled on the shelf! Farley wrote,

> *Wet sweetmeats must be kept in a dry and cool place, for a damp place will mould them, and a hot place will deprive them of their virtue. It is a good method to dip writing-paper into brandy, and lay it close to the sweetmeats. They should be tied well down with white paper, and two folds of cap-paper, to keep out the air, as nothing can be a greater fault than leaving the pots open or tying them down carelessly.*

2½ cups sugar

2 teaspoons pectin powder (available in supermarkets)

4 oranges, cut in half crosswise, pits removed

1 lemon, cut in half crosswise, pits removed

1 cup water

1 cup honey

1. In a small bowl, stir together the sugar and pectin. Set aside for later use.

2. Scoop out the flesh and pulp from the oranges and lemon with a melon baller or tablespoon. Place the pulp, juice, and flesh in a medium-sized pot. Slice the peel into ⅔-inch slivers, and reserve.

3. Add the water and honey to the pot, and stir to combine. Add the sugar-pectin mixture to the pot; stir to combine, and let stand for 2 minutes. Stir in the lemon and orange peel.

4. Wash down the sides of the pot with cool water and a pastry brush, making certain no sugar crystals remain. Bring the mixture to a boil, and cook, stirring occasionally, until thickened, 10 to12 minutes.

5. Remove from the heat and let cool completely. Transfer to an airtight container, and store in the refrigerator for up to 1 week.

GOOSEBERRY COMPOTE

MAKES 4 CUPS

Gooseberries and currants are closely related and share the same growing requirements. The bushes have thrived in England for centuries. Early cultures believed that fairies made their homes in the prickly bushes, so gooseberries were nicknamed "fayberries." The fruit was associated with magical powers to heal fevers and other illnesses, which modern scientists now attribute to its high levels of vitamin C. Try this compote on toast or with Mary Randolph's Shrewsbury Cakes (page 33) for a sweet boost of good health.

1½ cups water

1 cup granulated sugar

¼ cup orange juice

¼ cup orange liqueur (such as triple sec or Cointreau)

1 vanilla bean

1 tablespoon chopped fresh ginger

3 pints gooseberries, husked

¼ cup thinly sliced Candied Ginger (see page 191)

1. Prepare an ice bath (see Chef's Note, page 85).

2. In a large pot, place the water, sugar, orange juice, liqueur, vanilla bean, and fresh ginger. Stir to combine, and bring to a boil.

3. Add the gooseberries and cook, stirring occasionally, until the berries begin to pop, 5 to 7 minutes. Add the candied ginger and stir.

4. Transfer the compote to a stainless steel bowl, and set the bowl in the ice bath. Remove the vanilla bean, cool to room temperature, and store in an airtight container in the refrigerator for up to 1 week.

PINEAPPLE COMPOTE

MAKES 6 CUPS

Pineapples were fashionable because they were difficult to obtain and expensive in the American colonies. The tropical fruit became all the rage in European courts and kitchens. Josephine Bonaparte, originally from Martinique, craved this taste of home when she was empress of France and made the pineapple a staple of dinner at Napoleon's court. The fruit became so popular that pastry chefs molded cookies, candies, and gum paste to look like pineapples. There were pineapple-shaped cakes, gelatin, and ice cream molds.

1 pineapple
¼ cup golden rum
1 teaspoon cornstarch
2 cups pineapple juice
2 cups water
¼ cup granulated sugar
1 tablespoon whole allspice

1. Prepare an ice bath (see Chef's Note, page 85).

2. Trim the skin from the pineapple, remove the core, and cut the pineapple into ½-inch cubes.

3. In a small bowl, stir together the rum and cornstarch.

4. In a medium-sized pot, place the pineapple juice, water, and sugar; stir to combine, and bring the mixture to a boil. Add the allspice, and cook until the mixture reduces by half, about 5 minutes.

5. Add the rum-cornstarch mixture to the pot, stirring constantly. Add the pineapple and cook for just 1 minute.

6. Transfer the compote to a stainless steel bowl, and set the bowl in the ice bath. Cool to room temperature, and store in an airtight container in the refrigerator for up to 1 week.

STRAWBERRY JAM

MAKES 1¾ CUPS

Methods of canning were being developed in the late eighteenth century for Emperor Napoleon's army, but they were not known to cooks in America for decades. In 1790 Napoleon offered a cash prize to anyone who could develop a reliable method to keep food from spoiling on long voyages or on the battlefield. In 1806 Nicolas Appert successfully sealed meat and vegetables in glass jars and sent them safely to sea with the French navy.

4 cups strawberries, tops removed
½ cup sugar
3 tablespoons fresh lemon juice

1. Wash and dry the strawberries. Chop the berries coarsely, or pulse briefly in a food processor.

2. Transfer the berries and juices to a saucepan. Stir in the sugar and lemon juice.

3. Cook the mixture over medium heat, being careful of splattering berries and stirring frequently, until the jam is thickened and bubbles completely cover the surface, 9 to 10 minutes. Skim the surface, if necessary, with a slotted spoon.

4. Remove from heat and ladle into an airtight container. Store in the refrigerator for up to 2 weeks.

Acknowledgments

As in every work of my life, I want to thank my wife and business partner, Gloria, for her support.

To historian David McCullough, heartfelt thanks for his kind words and constant friendship. Thanks, too, to the many other scholars who helped me on my journey of mastering the cuisine of the eighteenth century, including Susan Schoelwer, Dr. Leni Sorenson, Susan Stein, and of course Bruce Cooper Gill. I would also like to recognize all the great minds in the U.S. Department of the Interior and the National Park Service for re-creating City Tavern so many decades ago and for assisting me as its proprietor and keeper. Special thanks go to the Independence National Historical Park for their research and dedication to bringing an accurate view of Revolutionary history to Philadelphia's visitors.

This book would not have been possible without City Tavern pastry chef Diana Wolkow. From the inception of the project she brought great skill and enthusiasm into our kitchens. Interpreting "receipts" from the 1700s and transforming them into successful modern-day recipes is no easy task. Diana tirelessly tested each recipe many times to assure they were accessible to modern bakers. She has all the precision of a scientist and the creativity of a great artist—the truly indispensable assets of an excellent pastry chef.

Pastry chef Robert Bennett's incredible sugar and chocolate work brought the look and spirit of the eighteenth century to life in the photos. He studied and re-created the eye-catching ornamental look of the sweet tables of the era and brought much to this project.

My gratitude goes to coauthor Molly Yun, who worked diligently and passionately on this project and drove it from inception to publication. Molly works with me daily at City Tavern and has immersed herself in the eighteenth century, from her study of costumes to cuisine. She brought her background in writing and journalism and her love of history to our offices and continues to inspire us.

Lastly, I would like to thank the entire staff of City Tavern for their constant commitment to re-creating an authentic eighteenth-century dining experience, and for all their behind-the-scenes help on this book.

Bibliography

Adams, Abigail. *New Letters of Abigail Adams, 1788–1801*. Edited by Stewart Mitchell. Boston: Houghton Mifflin, 1947.

Armes, Ethel, ed. and comp. *Nancy Shippen, Her Journal Book: the International Romance of a Young Lady of Fashion of Colonial Philadelphia*. Philadelphia: J. B. Lippincott, 1935.

Ayrton, Elisabeth. *The Cookery of England: Being a Collection of Recipes for Traditional Dishes of All Kinds from the Fifteenth Century to the Present Day, with Notes on Their Social and Culinary Background*. London: André Deutsch, 1974.

Beard, James. *James Beard's American Cookery*. Boston: Little, Brown, 1972.

Belden, Louise Conway. *The Festive Tradition: Table Decoration and Desserts in America, 1650–1900*. New York: W. W. Norton, 1983.

Bridenbaugh, Carl, ed. *Gentleman's Progress: The Itinerarium of Dr. Alexander Hamilton, 1744*. Chapel Hill: University of North Carolina Press for the Institute of Early American History and Culture at Williamsburg, 1948.

Bushman, Richard L. *The Refinement of America: Persons, Houses, Cities*. New York: Alfred A. Knopf, 1992.

Carson, Barbara G. *Ambitious Appetites: Dining, Behavior, and Patterns of Consumption in Federal Washington*. Washington, DC: American Institute of Architects Press, 1990.

Carter, Susannah. *The Frugal Colonial Housewife: A Cook's Book, wherein the Art of Dressing All Sorts of Viands with Cleanliness, Decency, and Elegance Is Explained*. Edited by Jean McKibbin. Garden City, NY: Doubleday, 1976. Originally published as *The Frugal Housewife, or Complete Woman Cook* (London: F. Newberry; Boston: Edes and Gill, 1772).

Cellania, Miss. "The Fight for Safe Milk: Pasteurization." Neatorama.com, 2011. www.neatorama.com/2011/01/24/the-fight-for-safe-milk-pasteurization/.

Child, Lydia Maria. *The American Frugal Housewife*. Facsimile of the 12th ed., 1833. Bedford, MA: Applewood, 1989.

Craughwell, Thomas J. *Thomas Jefferson's Crème Brûlée: How a Founding Father and His Slave James Hemings Introduced French Cuisine to America*. Philadelphia: Quirk, 2012.

Day, Ivan. *Cooking in Europe, 1650–1850*. Daily Life Through History series: Cooking Up History. Westport, CT: Greenwood Press, 2009.

Drinker, Elizabeth Sandwith. *The Diary of Elizabeth Drinker, Vol. 1*. Edited by Elaine Forman Crane. Boston: Northeastern University Press, 1991.

Escoffier, A. *The Escoffier Cookbook: A Guide to the Fine Art of Cookery*. 1941. New York: Crown, 1969. Originally published as *Le Guide Culinaire* (Paris, 1903).

Faber, Eli. *The Jewish People in America. Vol. 1, A Time for Planting: The First Migration, 1654–1820*. Baltimore: Johns Hopkins University Press, 1992.

Farley, John. *The London Art of Cookery and Housekeeper's Complete Assistant. 1783*. Edited by Ann Haly. Introduction by Stephen Medcalf. Lewes, England: Southover Press, 1988.

Fowler, Damon Lee, ed. *Dining at Monticello: In Good Taste and Abundance*. Chapel Hill: University of North Carolina Press, 2005.

Franklin, Benjamin. *The Autobiography of Benjamin Franklin, and Selections from His Other Writings*. Edited by Nathan G. Goodman. Philadelphia: University of Pennsylvania Press, 2005.

Glasse, Mrs. [Hannah]. *The Art of Cookery Made Plain and Easy*. Facsimile of the 1805 Alexandria ed. Introduction by Karen Hess. Bedford, MA: Applewood, 1997.

Herbst, Sharon Tyler. *Food Lover's Companion*. New York: Barron's, 1990.

Hines, Mary Anne, Gordon Marshall, and William Woys Weaver. *The Larder Invaded: Reflections on Three Centuries of Philadelphia Food and Drink*. Philadelphia: Library Company of Philadelphia, Historical Society of Pennsylvania, 1987.

Hooker, Richard J., ed. *A Colonial Plantation Cookbook: The Receipt Book of Harriott Pinckney Horry, 1770*. Columbia: University of South Carolina Press, 1984.

Kimball, Marie. *Thomas Jefferson's Cook Book*. Richmond, VA: Garrett & Massie, 1938.

Leighton, Ann. *American Gardens in the Eighteenth Century, "For Use or for Delight."* Boston: Houghton Mifflin, 1976.

Leslie, Eliza. *Directions for Cookery, in Its Various Branches*. Facsimile of the 1848 Philadelphia ed. Monterey, CA: Creative Cookbooks, 2001.

———. *Seventy-Five Receipts, for Pastry, Cakes, and Sweetmeats*. Facsimile of the 1st ed., 1828. Bedford, MA: Applewood, 1988.

Library of Congress. "Jump Back in Time: Revolutionary Period (1764–1789)." www.americaslibrary.gov/jb/revolut/jb_revolut_apple_1.html.

Lineback, Emily-Sarah, ed. *Preserving the Past: Salem Moravians' Receipts & Rituals*. Boonville, NC: Carolina Avenue Press, 2003.

Lowenstein, Eleanor. *Bibliography of American Cookery Books, 1742–1860*. 3rd ed. Worcester, MA: American Antiquarian Society, 1972.

Mariani, John. *The Encyclopedia of American Food and Drink*. New York: Lebhar-Friedman, 1999.

McLeod, Stephen, ed. *Dining with the Washingtons: Historic Recipes, Entertaining, and Hospitality from Mount Vernon*. Chapel Hill: University of North Carolina Press, 2011.

Meacham, Sarah Hand. *Every Home a Distillery: Alcohol, Gender, and Technology in the Colonial Chesapeake*. Baltimore: Johns Hopkins University Press, 2009.

Mintz, Sidney W. *Sweetness and Power: The Place of Sugar in Modern History*. New York: Viking, 1985.

Mount Vernon Memos. George Washington's Mount Vernon Estate and Gardens, Mount Vernon, VA.

Moxon, Elizabeth. *English Housewifry, Exemplified in Above Four Hundred and Fifty Receipts*. 9th ed., corrected. Leeds: George Copperthwaite, 1764.

Murrell, John. A *Daily Exercise for Ladies and Gentlewomen: Whereby They May Learne and Practise the Whole Art of Making Pastes, Preserues, Marmalades, Conserues, Tartstuffes, Gellies, Breads, Sucket-Candies, Cordiall Waters, Conceits in Sugar-Workes of Seuerall Kindes; As Also to Dry Lemonds, Orenges, or Other Fruits; Newly Set Forth According to the Now Approued Receipts Vsed Both by Honourable and Worshipfull Personages*. London, 1617.

Nutt, Frederick. *The Complete Confectioner; or, The Whole Art of Confectionary Made Easy*. 4th ed. New York: Richard Scott, 1807.

Ortiz, Elizabeth Lambert, ed. *The Encyclopedia of Herbs, Spices, and Flavorings: A Cook's Compendium*. New York: Dorling Kindersley, 1992.

Peckham, Howard H., ed. "Journal of Lord Adam Gordon." In *Narratives of Colonial America, 1704–1765*. Chicago: R. R. Donnelley & Sons, 1971.

Pennsylvania Gazette, June 12, 1766–July 4, 1792.

Platt, John D. R. *The City Tavern. Historic Resource Study*. Denver: National Park Service, U.S. Department of the Interior, 1973.

Raffald, Elizabeth. *The Experienced English Housekeeper*. Facsimile of the 1st ed., 1769. Introduction by Roy Shipperbottom. Lewes, England: Southover Press, 1997.

Randolph, Mary. *The Virginia House-Wife*. Facsimile of the 1st ed., 1824. Edited by Karen Hess. Columbia: University of South Carolina Press, 1984.

Rice, Kym S. *Early American Taverns: For the Entertainment of Friends and Strangers*. Chicago: Regnery Gateway, 1983.

Roberts, Kenneth, and Anna M. Roberts, eds. *Moreau de St. Méry's American Journey, 1793–1798*. Garden City, NY: Doubleday, 1947.

Rundell, Maria Eliza Ketelby. *A New System of Domestic Cookery: Formed upon Principles of Economy, and Adapted to the Use of Private Families throughout the United States, By a Lady*. New York: R. M'Dermut and D. D. Arden, 1814.

Schweitzer, Mary McKinney. "The Economy of Philadelphia and Its Hinterland." In *Shaping a National Culture: The Philadelphia Experience, 1750–1800*, edited by Catherine E. Hutchins, 99–119. Winterthur, DE: Henry Francis du Pont Winterthur Museum, 1994.

Sherrill, Charles H. *French Memories of Eighteenth-Century America*. New York: Charles Scribner's Sons, 1915.

Simmons, Amelia. *American Cookery*. Facsimile of the 2nd ed., 1796. Introduction by Karen Hess. Bedford, MA: Applewood, 1996.

Smith, Eliza. *The Compleat Housewife*. Facsimile of the 1758 London ed. London: Studio Editions, 1994.

Snyder, Rodney. "History of Chocolate: Chocolate in the American Colonies." Colonial Williamsburg, 2011. www.history.org/history/teaching/enewsletter/volume9/jan11/featurearticle.cfm.

Thompson, Mary V. "'Look Into the Milk and Butter': Food Preservation at George Washington's Mount Vernon." Department of the Registrar, Mount Vernon Ladies' Association, Mount Vernon, VA, January 1996.

Verral, William. *The Cook's Paradise: Being William Verral's 'Complete System of Cookery' Published in 1759 with Thomas Gray's cookery notes in Holograph*. Introduction and appendices by R. L. Mégroz. London: Sylvan Press, 1948.

Washington, Martha. *Martha Washington's Booke of Cookery*. Edited by Karen Hess. New York: Columbia University Press, 1995.

Williams, Sara Paston. *The Art of Dining: A History of Cooking and Eating*. London: Anova Books, 2012.

Index

A

Adams, Abigail, 14, 175
Adams, John, 2–3, 14, 70
ale
    about mead and, 2
    George Washington's Small Beer, 3
    Martha Custis Washington's Excellent
        Cake, 38–41
almonds. *See* nuts
amaretto, in Coffee Royale, 8–9
anise
    Fig and Anise Tart, 72–73
    Orange Anise Biscotti, 126–27
apples
    about: Johnny Appleseed and, 70
    Apple, Pear, or Quince Wine Preserves,
        211
    Apple and Fig Crumble, 54
    Apple Cranberry Cobbler, 55–56
    Johnny Appleseed's Pie, 70–71
    Strudel, 163–65
    See also cider
apricots
    about: Jefferson and, 124; Washingtons
        and, 124
    Almond Apricot Cookies, 124
    Apricot Fool, 102–3
    Apricot Preserves, 210
    Dried Cherry and Apricot Turnovers,
        159–61

B

Banana Nut Bread, 144–45
Bartram, John, 19, 58

beer, small, 3
Benjamin Franklin's Parmesan Cheesecake,
    19–20
berries
    Apple Cranberry Cobbler, 55–56
    Berry Gelée, 82–83
    Berry Preserves, 209
    Blackberry Almond Cheesecake, 21–23
    Blueberry Orange Trifle, 120–21
    Charlotte Russe, 110–12
    Corn Pudding with Strawberry Gelée,
        84–85
    Holiday Trifle, 118–19
    Orange Curd-Filled Meringue Cup with
        Berries, 166–67
    Peach and Raspberry Cobbler, 57
    Raspberry Champagne Shrub, 6–7
    Raspberry Charlotte Royale, 113–15
    Raspberry Pâte de Fruits, 186
    Raspberry Shrub, 207
    Raspberry Sorbet, 174
    Rhubarb and Strawberry Cobbler,
        58–59
    Strawberry Jam, 215
    Summer Berry Tart, 76–77
    Thaddeus Kosciuszko Tart, 64–65
    Vol-au-Vent with Berries, 157–58
beverages, 1–15
    about: ale and mead, 2; brandies, 1–2;
        cider, 2–3; historical perspective, 1–3;
        port, 1–2; wines and champagnes, 2
    Coffee Royale, 8–9
    Drinking Chocolate, 14–15
    Eggnog, 4–5

George Washington's Small Beer, 3
Raspberry Champagne Shrub, 6–7
Wassail, 10–11
West Indies Rum Punch, 12–13
biscotti, orange anise, 126–27
biscuits, sweet potato, 143
blackberries. *See* berries
Blair, Anne, 186
blancmange, vanilla bean, 88–89
blueberries. *See* berries
bourbon
    Chocolate Bourbon Pecan Tartlets,
       188–89
    Eggnog, 4–5
brandy
    about: historical perspective, 1–2
    Eggnog, 4–5
    Martha Washington's Great Cake,
       47–49
    Pear and Sour Cherry Cobbler, 53
    Syllabub, 204
    West Indies Rum Punch (peach brandy),
       12–13
breads. *See* quick breads

C

cakes, 17–49
    about: overview and historical
       perspective, 17–18
    Benjamin Franklin's Parmesan
       Cheesecake, 19–20
    Blackberry Almond Cheesecake, 21–23
    Charlotte Russe, 110–12
    Gingerbread, 24–25
    Hannah Glasse's Saffron Cake, 36–37
    Martha Custis Washington's Excellent
       Cake, 38–41
    Martha Washington's Chocolate Mousse
       Cake, 44–46

Martha Washington's Great Cake,
    47–49
Mary Randolph's Shrewsbury Cakes,
    33–35
Orange Glazed Almond Cake, 31–32
Plum Cake, 42–43
Pound Cake, 26–27
Ricotta Cheesecake, 28–30
Sugar Icing, 48
Vanilla Sponge Cake, 206
Candied Ginger, 191
Candied Pecans, 194
"Cannot Tell a Lie" Cherry Pie, 66–67
Carême, Marie-Antoine, 110, 157
champagne (sparkling wine)
    about: historical perspective, 2
    Champagne Gelée, 87
    Raspberry Champagne Shrub, 6–7
Chapman, John, 70
Charlotte Royale, Raspberry, 113–15
Charlotte Russe, 110–12
cheese
    Benjamin Franklin's Parmesan
       Cheesecake, 19–20
    Blackberry Almond Cheesecake, 21–23
    Parmesan Ice Cream, 178–79
    Ricotta Cheesecake, 28–30
cherries
    about: barrelling morello cherries, 159;
       drying, 53
    "Cannot Tell a Lie" Cherry Pie, 66–67
    Dried Cherry and Apricot Turnovers,
       159–61
    Pear and Sour Cherry Cobbler, 53
chestnuts. *See* nuts
Chocolate
    Chocolate Bourbon Pecan Tartlets,
       188–89
    Chocolate Ice Cream, 171

Banana Nut Bread, 144–45
Ginger Raisin Scones, 142
Pineapple Rum Bread, 146–47
Pumpkin Raisin Bread, 148–49
Sweet Potato Biscuits, 143
See also cakes
quinces
Quince, Currant, and Dried Fig
Turnovers, 162
Quince Wine Preserves, 211

R
Raffald, Elizabeth, 18, 61, 96
raisins
Ginger Raisin Scones, 142
Plum Pudding, 98–99
Pumpkin Raisin Bread, 148–49
See also currants
Randolph, Mary "Molly," 33, 137
raspberries. *See* berries
Rhubarb and Strawberry Cobbler, 58–59
Rice Pudding, 106–7
Ricotta Cheesecake, 28–30
rum
about: historical perspective, 2
Eggnog, 4–5
Pineapple Rum Bread, 146–47
Pumpkin Raisin Bread, 148–49
Rum Balls, 187
Spiced Red Currant Bread Pudding,
108–9
West Indies Rum Punch, 12–13

S
saffron
Hannah Glasse's Saffron Cake, 36–37
Saffron Mousse, 177
scones, ginger raisin, 142

sherry
Martha Custis Washington's Excellent
Cake, 38–41
Syllabub, 204
Shippen, Nancy, 192
Shrewsbury cakes, 33–35
shrub, raspberry, 207
Simmons, Amelia, 42, 56, 90
Smith, Eliza, 151–52, 183
Smith, Mary, 166
Snow Eggs, 96–97
sorbets. *See* ice creams and sorbets
Spice Cookies, 130
Spiced Candied Walnuts, 195
Spiced Red Currant Bread Pudding, 108–9
Spritz Cookies, 128–29
strawberries. *See* berries
streusel, oat and nut, 52
Strudel, 163–65
Summer Berry Tart, 76–77
Sweet Potato Biscuits, 143
sweetmeats. *See* petits fours and sweetmeats

T
tartlets. *See* petits fours and sweetmeats
tarts. *See* pies and tarts
Thaddeus Kosciuszko Tart, 64–65
Thomas Jefferson's Floating Island or Snow
Eggs, 96–97
Thomas Jefferson's Vanilla Bean Ice
Cream, 172
trifles, holiday, 118–19
turnovers. *See* pastries

V
vanilla
Thomas Jefferson's Vanilla Bean Ice
Cream, 172

About the Author

ABOUT CHEF WALTER STAIB

A third-generation restaurateur with more than four decades of culinary experience, Chef Walter Staib is an author, Emmy Award–winning TV host, James Beard–nominated chef, and culinary historian. He began his career in Europe, receiving formal training in many of Europe's finest hotels and restaurants, including Hotel Post, a historic five-star hotel in the Black Forest region of Germany, and Sommerberg Hotel in Wildbad, Germany. He also worked at the Chessery, one of Europe's premier hotels in Switzerland, hosting the likes of Elizabeth Taylor, Brigitte Bardot, and David Niven, as well as the Duke and Duchess of Windsor. This exclusive hotel had one of the most upscale restaurants in Europe, where Staib was offered a position because of his years of experience in kitchens, beginning as a child growing up and helping in a family-owned restaurant. He also worked at Switzerland's Casa Berno, owned by the Vatican, before coming to the United States in 1969. That's when he assumed a post as sous chef at the Mid America Club in Chicago and eventually served as Corporate Director of Food & Beverage Operations of the Omni Hotels chain.

As founder and president of Concepts By Staib, Ltd. (established 1989), a global restaurant management and hospitality consulting firm, Walter Staib has opened more than 650 restaurants worldwide. He is currently the driving force behind one of the nation's finest dining establishments, Philadelphia's City Tavern, a faithful recreation of an original eighteenth-century tavern and Concepts By Staib, Ltd.'s flagship operation.

In addition to being a top chef, restaurateur and consultant, Chef Staib has also authored several cookbooks. His first was *City Tavern Cookbook*. His follow-up cookbooks include: *City Tavern Baking & Dessert Cookbook*; *Black Forest Cuisine*, with recipes from his homeland; *The City Tavern Cookbook: Recipes from the Birthplace of America*; and *Feast of Freedom*, an illustrated children's book.

Walter Staib has made numerous appearances on local and national cooking shows, such as *60 Minutes*, the *Today* show, and the Food Network's *Best Thing I Ever Ate* and *Iron Chef*. He is the host of *A Taste of History*, which just received the 2012 James Beard Foundation nomination for Best TV Show on Location and was awarded four Emmy awards, including two as best host. The show is a vehicle for Staib to share eighteenth-century cuisine with a growing audience.

Chef Staib's culinary excellence has earned him numerous other awards, among them the prestigious Chevalier de l'Ordre du Mérite Agricole de la République Française, awarded in 1987. In 1996 he was also appointed the First Culinary Ambassador to the City of Philadelphia. In July 2006, he was named the Culinary Ambassador to the Commonwealth of Pennsylvania. The same year, he was also awarded the Seven Stars & Stripes Award for Excellence in Hospitality.

German President Dr. Horst Köhler conferred the Knight's Cross of the Order of Merit of the Federal Republic of Germany upon Staib in May, 2007. He also won the National Restaurant Association Keystone Humanitarian Award (Pennsylvania) that year. In 2008, the German-American Chamber of Commerce, Inc. granted him the Award of Leadership & Service. In 2009, he received Entrée of the Year by *Philadelphia* magazine. He was awarded the Silver Medal Award by the American Culinary Federation in 2010. The Colonial Society of Pennsylvania gave him the 2011 Contemporary Pioneer Award, and he was voted the Top Philadelphia Chef in the Condé Nast Cadillac Culinary Challenge in 2011. He was bestowed the Distinguished German-American of the Year in 2012 and won the regional 2012 Independent Restaurateur of the Year Award, and 2012 WHYY Best of the Chef Award.

ABOUT MOLLY YUN

An experienced journalist and food writer, Molly Yun writes about her love of the culinary arts, historical customs, and a variety of topics with readers in print and online. Her expertise in the culinary arts grew from a career as a professional cook and recipe developer, where she specialized in classic French and New American cuisine. She writes heart-healthy and historical recipes for Chef Walter Staib.

In addition, Molly has continued to pursue an interest in American history and material culture, including culinary traditions, clothing, and costuming. Her passion is to tell the real stories of the past through relatable subject matter. She researches and writes scripts for the PBS cooking show *A Taste of History*. Her theatrical script was seen on stage as part of the Philadelphia International Festival of the Arts.

She is the chair of the Young Friends of the Independence National Historical Park, a member of the Historic Foodways Society of the Delaware Valley, and a volunteer in historic hearth kitchens. Yun also sews her own eighteenth-century clothing from original patterns and consults as a historical costume specialist in interpreting fashions of the past.

Yun graduated magna cum laude from the University of Missouri, where she received the alumnus scholarship fellowship. As a journalist, she received the Delaware Business and Professional Women Young Careerist Award. She lives in Philadelphia with her husband Johnny, a chef. Together they enjoy experimenting in the kitchen with fresh ingredients from their garden.

ABOUT DIANA WOLKOW

Diana Wolkow is a pastry chef by profession and by nature. She loves to experiment with avant garde ingredients and ideas, while keeping composition simple, wholesome, and delicious.

Wolkow joined the City Tavern team as Executive Pastry Chef in 2010 after a year of international travels and real-world kitchen experience, where she collected inspiration and knowledge about the world's cuisines and inner workings of the industry. She operates a rigorous internship and training program to mentor budding pastry chefs in the Tavern's fast-paced and high-volume kitchen. There Wolkow also continues to perfect her approach of redesigning historic recipes for modern palates, drawing on her life of kitchen experience, travels, and her passion for dessert. Her pastries have been featured on *60 Minutes, The Best Thing I Ever Ate,* and the *Today* show, to name a few. Wolkow can also be seen cooking alongside Water Staib on *A Taste of History,* seen nationwide on PBS.

Originally from the Baltimore area, Wolkow moved to Philadelphia in 2005 to pursue her career in pastry art. She graduated summa cum laude from The Restaurant School at Walnut Hill College and has since greatly enjoyed being a part of the growing vibrant restaurant scene steeped in history in the city of brotherly love.